STOP TRYING
TO KEEP UP
WITH THE
JONE$ES

THEY'RE
BROKE
ANYWAY

STOP TRYING TO KEEP UP WITH THE JONE$ES

THEY'RE BROKE ANYWAY

A Financial Planner's Guide to Living Your Ideal Life

BRAD BERGER, CFP®, CLF®

Published by Advantage, Charleston, South Carolina.
Member of Advantage Media Group.

ADVANTAGE is a registered trademark and the Advantage colophon is a trademark of Advantage Media Group, Inc.

Printed in the United States of America.

Cornerstone Financial Strategies LLC
505 Broadway, Suite 400
Tacoma, WA 98402
(253) 756-2003
ContactUs@LiveYourIdealLife.com

ISBN: 978-159932-514-9
LCCN: 2015937794

This publication is designed to provide accurate and authoritative information in regard to the subject matter covered. It is sold with the understanding that the publisher is not engaged in rendering legal, accounting, or other professional services. If legal advice or other expert assistance is required, the services of a competent professional person should be sought.

Advantage Media Group is proud to be a part of the Tree Neutral® program. Tree Neutral offsets the number of trees consumed in the production and printing of this book by taking proactive steps such as planting trees in direct proportion to the number of trees used to print books. To learn more about Tree Neutral, please visit www.treeneutral.com. To learn more about Advantage's commitment to being a responsible steward of the environment, please visit www.advantagefamily.com/green

TABLE OF CONTENTS

ABOUT THE AUTHOR

Bradley A. Berger, CFP®, CLF®
Managing Partner and Owner
Cornerstone Financial Strategies, LLC

B rad is a CERTIFIED FINANCIAL PLANNER™ Professional and brings more than two decades of comprehensive financial planning experience to Cornerstone Financial Strategies. Previously, Brad served with an international financial planning firm starting in private practice and culminating a 17-year career as the Director of Advisor Operations. Recognizing that he wasn't living the advice he routinely gave to both clients and advisors to maintain a balanced and high quality of life, he decided to return to private practice in 2008 in order to spend more time with his family and in his community.

Brad enjoys helping people make smart choices about their money for the reasons that are important to them. This not only identifies long-range goals but also assists them in exploring the values upon which they are based. His clients appreciate the clarity and simplicity that come from working with a trusted advisor who serves as the head coach of their team of professionals, orchestrating the individual expertise of each subject matter specialist for their benefit. They also appreciate the coaching and accountability culture Brad brings to the implementation of the recommendations of the entire team. He wrote the foreword to an updated version of *Values Based Financial Planning—The Art of Creating an Inspiring Financial Strategy by Bill Bachrach*.

Brad is a Chartered Leadership Fellow from the American College. His education and training in the areas of personal and business finance, coupled with an extensive leadership background, makes him an ideal candidate for what he believes is essential in today's financial climate: having the ability to coordinate and orchestrate the necessary members of the client's Deliverables Team.

While developing, implementing, and coordinating the overall financial plan is Brad's specialty, he also has special expertise in the area of retirement planning and distribution as an Ed Slott Master Elite IRA Advisor. Brad is also an active member of the Tacoma Estate Planning Council and serves on the KBTC Association Board, and is a past member of the Professional Advisors Board of the Greater Tacoma Community Foundation.

Brad is a graduate of the United States Military Academy—West Point and served as an infantry officer in Berlin, Germany, during the fall of the wall. It is there that he met and married Theresa Buckley (a Department of Defense Dependent School Teacher originally from Wisconsin) in 1990. Theresa lost her battle to cancer in 2010. They had twin daughters together, Molly and Sarah. Brad and Theresa moved to University Place in 1998. Theresa was a beloved Reading Specialist for the University Place School District. The girls graduated from Curtis and were athletes on the Curtis Viking Swim Team, the Curtis Viking three time AAAA State Champion Water H.S. Polo Team (2007, 2008, 2009), and the Puget Sound Polo Junior Olympic Team. Molly and Sarah are graduates of the University of Portland. Molly graduated in 2014 with a bachelor of science in nursing, and Sarah graduated in 2015 with a double major in business marketing and operations technology management. Life has new beginnings as Brad is now happily married to Bethany Frymier Berger—an Enterprise Project Manager in a large telecom company. They live in Bellevue with their two sons, Braxton and Bennett, yellow lab Zeus, and the girls when they are home to visit. Braxton and Bennett attend Puesta del Sol—Bellevue Public School District's Spanish Immersion Program. The entire family enjoys Disney, winter skiing at White Pass (where Brad is a Volunteer Alpine Ski Patroller), and summers on Lake Entiat, Lake Chelan, and Lake Washington. Brad is an instrument-rated private pilot (land and float) and also enjoys scuba diving—ask him about the Manta Rays of Hawaii!

Email Brad at ContactUs@LiveYourIdealLife.com

ENSEMBLE PRACTICE ADVANTAGE

In today's turbulent and complex economy, you simply can't leave your dreams and desires to chance. The days of the "solo" practitioner have been eclipsed by the increasing complexities of our lives. In our opinion, it is simply impossible for a financial planner to be competent and effective in every aspect of financial, legal, and life planning.

In our ensemble model, we bring you more than 55 years of hands-on experience in the team members of Bill Pickles, Brad

Berger, and Mike Pickles. And though each has knowledge of and experience with almost every facet of financial planning, each specializes in a distinct discipline. We operate as a team—with each member responsible for primary tasks. Bill, Brad, and Mike have extensive experience in business planning, succession planning, retirement income distribution, and risk management—this makes them an ideal choice for complex case design. Bill's experience in Institutional Money Management positions him distinctly as our primary coordinator of wealth management solutions. Brad's background in comprehensive financial planning situates him for the coordination and implementation process. Mike's vast experience in both retail and institutional client service enables a flexible support component for the needs of both our clients and our team.

But this is simply not enough! This is why, despite the considerable experience of Cornerstone Financial Strategies' team, and the independence, support, and backing of LPL Financial, we rely on the services of additional professionals to bring you advice that will help you on your financial journey. This approach is what we believe separates us from the other choices you have and what will give you the highest probability of aligning your most important goals with your most deeply held values.

We have access to a team of specialists in a wide variety of disciplines. These individuals and firms are not affiliated with our firm but have been carefully screened and have passed our rigorous standards for skills, ethics, professionalism, and client service. All understand our process and services, and many have experienced the Financial Road Map® process for themselves. Since we consider ourselves "Life Planners" who specialize in money, and the fact that quality of life extends well beyond the financial world, our list is not limited to only attorneys, CPAs, mortgage brokers, real estate professionals, lenders, and trust officers. It also includes physicians, dentists, travel agents, contractors, professional clothiers, professional organizers, and other service professionals. Of course, you, as the client, always have the final decision. We are willing to coordinate with anyone you are either currently working with or may choose in the future.

Additionally, we rely on the coaching assistance and guidance of other nationally recognized professionals to keep us up-to-date and at the top of our game for the benefit of our clients. These resources go well beyond a newsletter subscription or access to a website. These are individuals that we have a personal, ongoing relationship with and immediate access to. In addition to e-mail and teleconference, we also train with them regularly face-to-face.

Finally, we rely on the expertise of the Cornerstone Financial Strategies Advisory Board that consists of selected clients and local business leaders. Our semi-annual meetings provide an excellent exchange of ideas and recommendations of how we can improve our effectiveness and enhance the client experience.

INTRODUCTION

FAR MORE THAN INVESTING

"Dad, can you talk to my nursing class about money?"

My daughter Molly was nearing graduation at the University of Portland and was concerned that she and her classmates didn't know enough about finances. "We don't know what the real world will be like."

"What are you interested in learning?" I asked.

As it turned out, Molly was interested in what you'd expect college students to be worried about—loans, loan consolidation, and interest rates—"and how do I make sure that I am successful financially?"

I have spent nearly 25 years helping financial clients, families, and businesses plan for retirement, so this was a perfect opportunity to speak to her and other young people at the start of their careers. Besides, it was one of the first times my daughter had sought out my advice as an adult, so I had no intention of turning her down.

I presented a 90-minute talk, followed by about an hour of questions and answers. Afterward, one of the graduating students told me, "I've been here four years, and no one has ever talked to us about money. That was the best class I've ever been to."

My daughter was pleased, too. "I had no idea you knew so much about money, Dad!"

I had to smile—what did she think I did for a living? I've been a financial planner as long as she's been alive. But it also made me think: with so many different jobs in the financial services industry, it's hard to know exactly which services "financial planners" should, or even actually do, provide.

A key reason that I decided to write this book is that the public needs to know more about what a financial planner should do and why every family needs a good one. If I were to ask a hundred people their definition of financial planning, I would get a hundred different responses. Most would talk about stocks, bonds, and mutual funds management. Few would get to the core of it.

The financial media have conditioned the public to believe that financial planning is synonymous with stock market investing and performance. Yes, investing is an important element of financial planning—but it is only one of five disciplines in a truly comprehensive strategy. You also need to manage risks, plan for life in retirement, develop a comprehensive tax plan, and put in place a plan to help your family after you are gone.

This book will examine those disciplines—as well as the principle of values-based financial planning, which is central to the philosophy of my firm, Cornerstone Financial Strategies.

I have been a husband and father, for better or worse, in sickness and in health. My two daughters, Molly and Sarah, both inspiring young women, have graduated from college and launched their careers. We lost their mother, Theresa, to cancer almost five years ago, but we have since been blessed with a larger family: I have remarried, and Beth is an amazing woman, as are her two young boys, Braxton and Bennett, who now are my sons as well.

Like every family, we have many goals and dreams, and they have inspired us to take the steps needed to reach them. We have examined our values to make sure they are aligned with our intentions. I have learned that the accumulation of shiny objects does not lead to happiness. Nothing is wrong with having a nice home and car and providing a good education for your children—but I strongly believe that first we should examine the "why" behind the "what."

Before you do or buy or plan anything, you should ask yourself why—and whether you are meeting the standards you have set for yourself and your family. I would like to help you identify what your family's dreams might be and to start planning together to make them happen.

You should strive to you live your Ideal Life through a process that:

- Aligns your financial choices with your most important goals and your most deeply held values.
- Gets your entire financial house in order and keeps it that way forever.
- Gives you confidence that no matter what happens in the markets, the economy, or the world, you will be on track toward your goals.
- Frees up mental and physical space and time so that you can focus on the things in your life that are more important than money.

PART ONE

THE SUCCESS FUNDAMENTALS

Sometimes a quote is frequently repeated because it so succinctly captures a truth, and here's one from hockey star Wayne Gretzky that can be applied to many things in life, among them investing: "I skate to where the puck is going, not to where it has been."

In the early years of my financial services career that now has spanned almost a quarter-century, the market seemed unstoppable. Yes, there were some down periods, but the recovery was swift. I recall many talks with clients whose focus seemed to be on all the talk around the water cooler. A week didn't go by without at least one client pointing out the uptick in some coworker's portfolio. They mostly were concerned that their investment was getting trounced by somebody else's—not whether the investment was helping to reach their goals.

It was a classic case of trying to keep up with the Joneses.

The fundamental problem with chasing market performance is that by the time you recognize that a particular investment has been doing well, you likely will be too late to participate in the gain. It's more likely that you will buy too high, and you could be in for a great fall.

Success has little to do with beating some benchmark or index, and it has even less to do with what your neighbor's stocks are doing.

An ideal life is so much more, and it depends on the individual. You need your own index for success: What do you need to achieve in order to attain the life you want to live? If you're living your ideal life in retirement, it is unlikely that people will be asking you, "So, what was your rate of return?" They are more likely to want to know the steps you took to attain the lifestyle you are enjoying.

It comes down to this: Given your resources and what you want to achieve, can you get from where you are today to where you need to be? The rate of return is not as important as you might think. Keeping up with the Dow Jones Industrial Average or with the Standard & Poor's 500 index may not be what you need to do. You may need to do a little more—but you may also need to do less.

One reason that people don't do as well as they could is that they do not truly understand the impact of risk and volatility. No one ever complains about the upside volatility. They complain about the downside. Seeking those big returns, they take too much risk and then get burned, taking their money out of the market at the wrong time.

The financial plans that we design are first and foremost based on what is important to you—your goals, your dreams, your values. We then examine how much risk is appropriate and acceptable to you and how much of a return you truly need to meet each goal at the right time.

CHAPTER 1

IN PURSUIT OF VALUES

I t took me years to figure out what was really important to provide to clients. After I graduated from West Point and served our nation as an army infantry officer, I worked for an international financial planning firm that did planning for members of the military. My financial advising career grew from advisor to branch manager to district manager to regional director to divisional director. In my almost 18 years there, I managed hundreds of advisors and even more clients.

That's when I was introduced to values-based financial planning. We developed a "financial road map" to define deeply held values and goals before developing savings, allocation, or asset plans. My accountability coach and I reviewed my own roadmap every two weeks to make sure my financial action steps were aligned with my values and goals.

It dawned on me in one of these sessions that I was not living in alignment with my values. I'd become a workaholic and was traveling constantly. I was responsible for all of our district offices west of the Rockies, including operations in Asia, the Hawaiian Islands, Guam, and Okinawa, and so I was on the road two days out of three. I wanted to grow in my career, but I was craving time with my family. I was a successful senior-level executive, but success in corporate America demands significant sacrifice. I lost more and more of my free time. I missed major events in my family's life. I was not home for anniversaries. I was not home for birthdays. I missed some of my daughters' water polo games.

This focus on purpose and meaning helped me to take the right planning steps to get the results that reflected my most closely held goals and objectives. I wanted to apply this process to our clients so that they, too, could meet their most meaningful goals in life with financial support in place.

Even though the company had introduced values-based planning to the entire field force and was initially willing to train the company in it's application, it quickly discovered the effort it would take by everyone in the organization. Despite their efforts, I did not believe it was truly interested in pursuing such values-based planning. Corporately, they were simply unwilling to do the work the goal required. It ultimately returned to a comfortable, known approach to help it meet its earnings goals, and I felt the focus on revolutionizing their approach was lost. Sure, profitability and asset growth are important for financial services companies, but I saw a huge gap in how to optimize meeting clients' individual priorities.

I felt that there must be a better way. If the company was not going to embrace values-based financial planning, then I would do so myself. I knew that I could build a practice employing it. After all those years with the company, I needed to make a change for my family and my clients. It was time for me to go.

I soon joined Cornerstone Financial Strategies, a values-based financial planning practice, which I eventually purchased with a partner. My firm now helps clients understand what is most important to them and define their goals. We then develop customized plans that coordinate investments and risk management, in concert with legal and tax considerations.

We work with a team of professionals, including attorneys, accountants, insurance specialists, and wealth managers. Together, we find unified and cohesive strategies that address our clients' needs and goals—and we check in with them quarterly, so that their plans evolve as life changes. We are, indeed, a "cornerstone" in our clients' lives, but it's about more than money. It's about values.

"When your values are clear, your decisions are easy," the late Roy Disney was credited as saying. I was at that crossroads when I decided to launch out on my own. As a trainer and mentor, I had been encouraging advisors to build successful practices. I had a passion for it. I had the confidence and the tools to return to private practice myself. The decision was easy because I had absolute clarity of my values at that point. Hard work lay ahead—but the decision itself was easy. I knew I could make a difference.

I knew that I could build a successful practice based on my values—on family, on faith, on friends, on what matters to me in life. At my fork in the road, I chose the right direction. Values-based financial planning is what people want. They crave something better, something meaningful.

I pride myself in being the type of leader who gets involved and puts his values into action. I want to be known as someone who walks his talk. It wasn't long after I went into private practice that I was put to the test. I was not anticipating the crisis that would hit my family. I was expecting to grow old with Theresa, but I was all the more ready to handle her death now that I was focusing on my family and my values.

A BASIS FOR SOUND DECISIONS

When the unexpected happened, my family already had a comprehensive financial plan in place. I believe in the principles advocated by Bachrach & Associates, Inc., headed by Bill Bachrach, who conceived the concept of the Financial Road Map®. His mission was to create a corps of qualified advisors who practice values-based financial planning.

If you come to suspect that your financial choices are out of alignment with your goals, you will be served best by an advisor who has been trained in values-based financial planning. The Financial Road Map® process helps you uncover and articulate the values you already possess. I provide every one of my clients with a copy of Bachrach's book, *Values-Based Financial Planning*.

The people who are the best fit for our firm are financial delegators: They leave the financial micromanaging to professionals and focus instead on friends, family, community, hobbies, travel, and enjoying their lives.

Above all, they are passionate about their goals. They realize that achieving financial security and an enhanced quality of life requires commitment, money, time, and planning. They are ready to hear the truth about their financial situation and are committed to doing the work their goals require.

They are willing to accept advice. They value the teamwork and accountability that comes from a structured plan of action and the professional follow-up that successful results will require. They understand the value of true professionals and are comfortable with compensating them for their expertise. They appreciate the clarity and simplicity that come from working with a trusted advisor who serves as the head coach of their team of professionals.

I strive to understand what's important to my clients about money, about life, and about values. I am not attempting to change their values. I'm not trying to talk them into something they don't believe; rather, I am helping them to articulate what they do believe and to get that down on paper in an organized manner.

Everybody has values, but it can be difficult to succinctly or eloquently express those values in a way that could become a map for life. That's what I help them to do. I meet with couples who have been married for decades, and for many it's the first time they have ever talked together about "the why behind the what." I help them bring to the surface and into the light the values that play into why they do the things they do and what drives them. Then I help to translate those values into tangible and measurable goals. Those, in turn, become the basis for all decisions.

I start with the question, "What's important about money to you?" Whatever the response, we dig deeper. Here's a typical conversation with a client:

"What's important about money to you?"

"Having enough of it."

"What's important about having enough of it to you?"

"Well, I want to make sure I'm meeting all my financial obligations."

"What's important about meeting all of your financial obligations to you?"

"Because that's what I need to do to be a good dad and husband."

By drilling down to what motivates each response, we can quickly uncover clients' core values. We see how they view money, and that plays an important role in customizing a financial plan.

Articulating Your Values

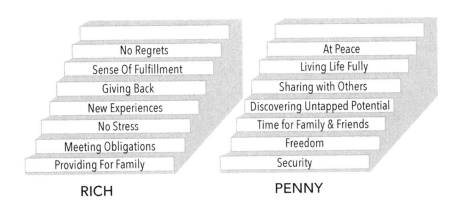

RICH

PENNY

The discovery of those values is the first step of a four-part framework for true financial planning, which we'll examine in the next chapter. Above all, I am trying to help you see your finances in a rounded way with all the elements needed to lead a fulfilling life. I'm helping them develop a framework for success.

It is important to understand what drives your decisions. My own financial roadmap and values staircase have given me clarity. I understand why I do what I do and what is behind my decisions—and I regularly double check whether an action is in alignment with what is important to me. In other words, I ask whether my action is in keeping with my values or takes me further away from them.

You need to be constantly reevaluating as life changes. In my case, for example, Theresa's death changed the trajectory of my life and what became important to me. For decades while we were married, my priority was accumulating for that almighty retirement. We sacrificed a lot of things along the way for that one particular goal.

I see now how fragile life can be. It can be taken from us at any point in time. I have decided to start living more in the moment, for today, striking a balance between making sure that I will have a secure, comfortable retirement and also making sure I'm enjoying life as I go, supporting both needs and goals.

CHAPTER 2

A FRAMEWORK FOR SUCCESS

I have fond memories of my mother and my grandparents taking care of me. My mother was young, single, and worked as much as she could to provide for me. My grandfather was a retired navy chief, and my grandmother was a pioneer in her career—inspirational, outspoken, and hard working. Those were the values that I was raised with. The philosophy was if you want to do it, you simply have to figure out a way to make it happen.

I was born in 1965. My mother was young. That was a time when I'm sure she endured a significant amount of judgment, and yet my mother, along with my grandparents, raised me. My mother later remarried when I was eight and I had a father I knew for the first time.

In retrospect, I would say we were a lower-middle-class family, and yet I thought I had it pretty good, particularly in comparison to many of my friends. It was the life I knew. My family provided me with the basics, but I knew that I would have to work for the extras in life, and I was encouraged to do so. And so, I had a paper route. I mowed lawns.

My parents chuckled when I told them that I wanted to learn to fly. Yes, I could get my pilot's license, they told me—if I could figure out how to pay for it. And I did. At the age of 17, I had my private pilot's license. It was one of my greatest early achievements. Another was my ability to ski which I paid for myself. We lived 13 miles from Mission Ridge on the eastern side of the Cascades in Washington State, and I was able to ski three to four days a week during my high school years. Today, I'm a volunteer ski patroller, using that skill for the benefit of others as a way to give back.

And so, encouraged by my family, I was able to pursue those passions. But I knew that my parents would not be able to pay to send me to college. That was clear. We lived well enough, but they couldn't afford to buy expensive cars, and they certainly couldn't send a kid to college. I knew I was going to have to figure that out on my own. That's when I started to pursue scholarship opportunities. I didn't want to work my way through college; I wanted college itself to be my work.

The educational benefits were one reason that I looked into entering one of the service academies—although I had military role models in my life who played into that decision. My grandfather was a retired navy chief. My father was a retired E-8 in the army. It was a lifestyle I was familiar with.

What my parents had was fine, but I wanted more in my life—and so I put into action their advice that I could have whatever I wanted if

I could just figure out a way to make it happen. It required planning and research. It required exploration of options to determine the best course of action, weighing the pros and cons.

So many people think they need to live the life that someone else prescribes for them. They haven't examined their own unique situation, evaluated their own values, discovered their dreams, or pursued their goals. They seem to care more about image and the accumulation of things.

Life shouldn't be about trying to keep up with the Joneses—in my experience, they're broke anyway. The people who you think have money (based on the cars they drive, the clothes they wear, the homes they live in, the vacations they take, and the toys they have) may be living paycheck to paycheck, accumulating very little to fund even a meager lifestyle in retirement. Sometimes, those that appear as the "millionaires next door" are an illusion. They may make a lot of money and live extravagantly, but they are spending all of their effort and energy on today. They are saving nothing for the future.

You should seek out qualified and experienced advice for your financial planning, but no financial prescription fits all people. Your values may lead you to decisions that others might find questionable. I recently met with a great couple who have made some financial choices that, if you were to evaluate them only superficially, you might think unwise. But when you take it into the context of their values and what they hold dear, those decisions are in complete alignment.

I think much of the American public has been convinced that the only way to achieve financial success is to beat the market. That is not true. The secret to success is determining what you want to achieve and then figuring out what it's going to take to achieve that. That, essentially, is the principle that my parents instilled in me.

Living in alignment with one's values does not automatically bring on the good life, but it becomes the foundation that informs your decisions on what you wish to pursue. Then, from that foundation, you can figure out whether it is achievable and how.

That is what I help people to do: I help them decide what works for them and what is best for them. If you wish to keep up with the Joneses, you must ask yourself whether you are being realistic. Is it something you are able to achieve? And even if it is, do you truly want to achieve it? Each decision should be run through the filter of your values.

THE FOUR ELEMENTS OF THE FRAMEWORK

In short, financial planning strives to help you live your ideal life. At this point, you may be convinced that you have to start doing something—but what might that be? Let's talk about the four components of the framework for success. They are: discovery, planning, solutions, and monitoring.

Some people in the financial services industry are focused on the sale and distribution of products while some will work with clients to write financial plans, but they do not implement them or coordinate them with the other disciplines of planning. Then there are some that offer a truly comprehensive financial plan: They help their clients discover their values, define their goals, review their planning options, implement strategies to meet those goals, and monitor the results. It is a coordinated approach in which subject matter experts collaborate on financial planning, risk and wealth management, and tax and legal issues.

Some of the financial industry focuses on the "solutions" aspect of the framework—that is, specific products that may or may not meet the goals and timing that the client hopes to achieve. Customers end up feeling that they are being sold something. They become defensive and numb to the sales pitches, which ignore the discovery, planning, and monitoring phases. (A note here about the difference between a client and a customer. I have always felt that customers are people who buy something, whereas clients are lifelong relationships. At Cornerstone, we don't have hundreds or thousands of customers, but we have dozens of clients. This allows us to provide the level of service our style of financial planning and monitoring requires.)

As I tell clients, everything looks like a nail if your only tool is a hammer. A lot of the people in the financial services industry have only a hammer. They have specific products to sell, so they present them as the perfect solution for you. But many tools can meet a client's goals: stocks, bonds, mutual funds, REITs (Real Estate Investment Trust), annuities, insurance, real estate, commodities, futures, ETFs (Exchange Traded Funds), precious metals—the list goes on and on.

Instead of jumping to some "solution" that may not serve you best, you and your planner should spend a lot of time in the other phases: discovery, planning, and monitoring. The solutions, while important, are just a sliver of the process.

In the **discovery phase**, we use the Financial Road Map® to help clients articulate their values. Then we help them establish goals and milestones for reaching them. How will they feel when they achieve them? When do they want to attain a particular goal, and how much money will that require? We look at their current financial situation to assess the possibilities.

It's important to focus on the "why" of financial planning before considering the "what." A computer can calculate the what, but it cannot tell you the why. It cannot define your personal values and your goals—and unless those are established first, how can you know that a specific solution is appropriate for you? In working with clients, I ask them to fast-forward and picture themselves as having achieved a goal. I ask them to describe in a few words what they are thinking and feeling now that they have arrived. That's the "why." That is what the planning will provide for them.

The **planning phase** itself is quite detailed. We want to make sure the right product is used for the right job. In my opinion, there are no bad financial products, but there are many financial products applied badly. Financial regulations keep these products out of the marketplace unless they have been vetted—at least somewhat. But such oversight tends to break down when it comes to whether the products are being used for the purpose for which they were designed. You could hammer in a screw as if it were a nail, but in doing so you would be misusing both the hammer and screw.

When finding a potential **solution**, we collect all the pertinent numbers and review them, and we talk about approaches and products. We need to uncover whether the client would object to a particular strategy. There often is an alternative—not the ideal one, perhaps, but one that will get the job done. But before abandoning what we believe will provide the best outcome, we want to understand the reason for the objection. Was it a bad experience? Was it something they heard? We want to get to the source of why a client wouldn't feel comfortable with a particular strategy.

Annuities, for example, are a hot topic. Some people love them, some hate them. In truth, they are simply a tool. Is term insurance the right solution for everybody? No. Is it the right solution for some? Sure. Others would be served best by whole life insurance or some other product. Still, people often have misgivings based on their own or other people's experiences. We talk about those impressions, and seek to understand where they are coming from. Was it a case of a product applied badly? Or might the client simply need more information?

As an independent financial planner, I can offer my clients access to a wide array of products and strategies. Unlike some advisors, I am not beholden to any particular firm or to any product line. I can choose anything. I can choose from the universe of products and tools that are available. If the client is adamant about not pursuing a particular strategy, I'll offer more information and, if necessary, a different solution.

There are many considerations when building a financial plan, including diversifying risk, minimizing taxes for you or your heirs, investment choices, allocation strategies, liquidity concerns, time horizons, and legal considerations now and in the future. The client has the final word.

In the **monitoring phase**, we review more than 150 checkpoints for our clients during the course of a year. Many may not apply to a client at a particular point in time, if ever. Nonetheless, the financial team considers how each one might apply and how we would deal with it. The monitoring phase is critically important, and it has become more complex. Life's pace is faster. People are subject to more rules and regulations, which can provide many opportunities but also present a lot of potential pitfalls.

The checklist looks into the various aspects of tax and legal planning, which I will discuss in detail in later chapters. We do an all-risks review that includes not only the traditional risk elements but also considers your insurance coverage, your protection from cyber crime, and whether you have systems in place to back up your photographs, documents, spreadsheets, and contact lists. Our monitoring checklist also includes your credit status and the suitability of your business structure, if applicable. Are you sufficiently protected from liability? Are you protected from identity theft? Have you backed up your electronic data? Does your partner know all of your usernames, passwords, site keys, and challenge questions—or at least where the list is that contains all of this information?

EN ROUTE TO YOUR IDEAL LIFE

Our clients tell us that they appreciate that we're truly looking out for them. The elements of discovery, planning, solutions, and monitoring help our clients get their entire financial house in order and keep it that way. It doesn't happen overnight. It can take months, or even years, and we revisit the plan regularly. We want to do everything possible to make sure their financial plans run smoothly.

Financial planning is not a destination; it is a journey. I am constantly monitoring and tweaking my own plan. As I accomplish goals, I regularly add new ones. I adjust to changes in the market and to estate laws and taxes. The plan evolves as my family needs change. There is always some way to improve it.

About 95 percent of a financial plan tends to remain consistent. It's that final 5 percent that takes the tweaking. But we need to pay careful attention to those details, because that's what can derail a financial plan. Those details include maximizing retirement savings, attending to changes in beneficiaries and powers of attorney, keeping track of the growth and size of the estate, and monitoring distributions from qualified plans.

It's like navigating a ship. Getting to the destination requires frequent minor adjustments. If the crew doesn't attend to those corrections constantly, the ship could wind up far astray, without sufficient fuel or time to get back on course.

Our desire is to help you live your Ideal Life. We believe the way to do that is to align your financial choices with your most important goals and your most deeply held values. Once your financial house is in order, you will gain confidence regardless of what happens in the markets, the economy, or the world. No matter what the Joneses are doing, you will be on track toward your own goals. You will be able to focus on the things in life that are more important than money.

CHAPTER 3

OVERRATED RATE OF RETURN

Your colleague at the water cooler, Ken Jones, starts bragging one day about how great a performance he has seen with one of his investments. "You should check out that rate of return!" Ken says. "Sure, there are some off years, but wow just look at how well it's done on the average."

Numbers, as we all know, can be deceptive at first glance.

Let's say that Ken has an investment that starts out with $10,000. Now, imagine an amazingly good year. It goes up 100 percent, and he has $20,000. The next year is horrible: Ken takes a 50 percent hit. That means after two years of investing, Ken is back where he started at $10,000.

So what was Ken Jones' average annual rate of return? Well, the average of those two percentages is a 25 percent gain. That is, 100 minus 50 divided by 2 equals 25. So Ken could go tell his friends he posted a 25 percent return. He might not want to add that he has nothing to show for it. He hasn't earned a cent. Meanwhile, Rich's investment earned 6 percent in each of those two years. Its average return was 6 percent, far less than that wondrous 25, but it earned far better than zero. Using the compound interest table on page 56 Rich's investment would be $11,200 in this example ($10,000 x 1.12)

The same can be true of chasing performance:

In the example on the following page, $458.33/month is invested in two different markets. Market "A" has a steady and consistent climb, while market "B" trends down and then back near it's starting point (sideways if you will). Market "A" reflects a higher rate of return for the period ($23 - $12 / $12 = 91.67%), yet market "B", with a negative rate of return for the period ($10 - $12 / $12 = -16.67%), had a higher ending value.

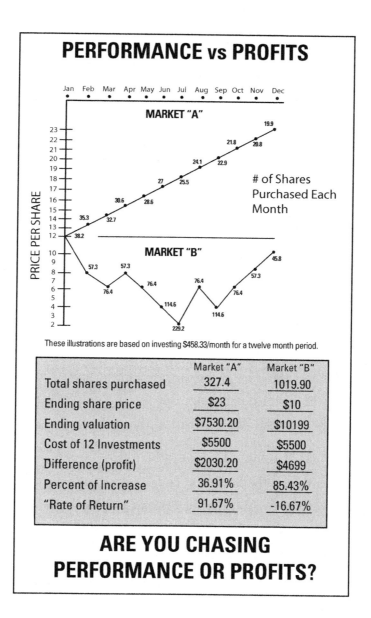

PERFORMANCE vs PROFITS

These illustrations are based on investing $458.33/month for a twelve month period.

	Market "A"	Market "B"
Total shares purchased	327.4	1019.90
Ending share price	$23	$10
Ending valuation	$7530.20	$10199
Cost of 12 Investments	$5500	$5500
Difference (profit)	$2030.20	$4699
Percent of Increase	36.91%	85.43%
"Rate of Return"	91.67%	-16.67%

ARE YOU CHASING
PERFORMANCE OR PROFITS?

If you retired in 2007, began withdrawing from your investments, and a market crash was the first thing you experienced, you'd be in much worse shape than someone with the same investment who retired two years later and the market went up. This is because constant dollar withdrawals in a declining market would represent a larger proportion of your investment as compared to the same constant dollar withdrawal schedule in a rising market. But from the perspective of average return a decade later, both scenarios could result in very similar calculated rates of return.

Beware of the impacts of "sequence of return." The timing of your good and bad years makes a major difference. But by any name, it's common sense. The math doesn't lie. So before you let yourself be wowed by an investment's average annual return over the past decade, ask some questions. These might include what is the year-over-year rate of return, how consistent has it been, and what is the volatility?

We all know the story of the tortoise and the hare. The media love the hare. The tortoise is boring. But we all know who wins in the end. Steady and slow. The race isn't to the swift.

That is why I think you need to be focused less on whether the rate of return beat the S&P 500 and focused more on whether you achieved your goals. You should be asking: "Did I take the level of risk that I needed to take, given the resources that I had, to achieve the goals that I set out for myself?"

Volatility can be particularly dangerous in a down market. What we really need to do is dampen volatility, because it's far better to get a 6 percent rate of return year after year than to be bouncing all over the place—up 24, down 36, up 48, down 24, up 12, as indicated in the following chart:

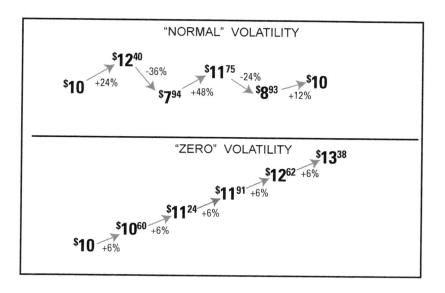

Roller coasters are much alike. They go around in a big circle. They go up and down. Some give the riders a bigger thrill, with higher ups and deeper downs, but they all are based on momentum and gravity, starting at one point and ending, safely, at another.

The market is not a whole lot different. You have to determine what kind of ride you want to go on during this particular time of your life. What's more important? If you have a choice in determining the same end result, how is it that you want to get there? How will you feel when you return to the platform?

There tends to be overemphasis on rate of return as I believe the concept of consistent compounding is either under valued or perhaps misunderstood. I would much prefer a steady rate of return year after year without volatility (as pictured in the lower pane of the example above). Every compound interest table or financial calculator that is found online is built upon zero volatility. It's based upon a consistent rate of return.

If that's how you actually achieve those results, then that calculator makes sense for you. But we all should know that's not the way the economy has ever worked. You can expect a big correction every so often.

You may like the thrill of a roller coaster, particularly when you're young and your stomach can take it, but do you want that sinking sensation in your gut when it comes to your investments? After a roller coaster ride, you can regain your footing in a few moments. In the world of investments, it might take years to recover from a wild ride, if you ever do.

THE PROPER EMPHASIS

In their order of significance, these are the six important elements of the success fundamentals:

1. How early you start investing
2. How often you invest
3. How much you invest
4. Whether you stay invested
5. How much you keep (avoiding tax erosion)
6. Your rate of return

You will note that your rate of return is not number 1. In fact, although it qualifies as important, it's last on that list. Don't be obsessed with chasing performance. Instead focus on putting a plan together that considers every element.

One of my business partners came from a world of institutional money management. At that level, his responsibility was, essentially, comparing quarterly performance on investments down to the tenth of a percent. It didn't result in wealth, just comparison.

That was a miserable perspective, he decided. He found it far more compelling to hear the stories of how people had achieved their wealth. Those stories reveal that gaining wealth has a lot less to do with rate of return than it does with behavior and choices.

Notice that the first five elements of the success fundamentals are behaviorally driven. It's only the sixth one, the rate of return that an individual doesn't influence directly. It is dependent on business and industry conditions, the economic winds, international relations, and prevailing perceptions, to name a few.

There is a science and an art behind rate of return. You do have some control, such as the investment you choose, the asset classes you participate in, and how the money is diversified. You can, potentially, influence the outcome through a series of smart choices—but that's not the same as saying you have control.

You are, however, in full control of how early you start, how often you invest, how much you invest, whether you stay invested or not, and the taxable nature of the account (taxable, tax-deferred, or tax free). Focusing on those is how you can build wealth. The rate of return does indeed matter, but it's folly to put your emphasis on beating some index by a fraction. If it's down 25 percent and your investment is down only 24.5, will you be celebrating?

THE COST OF PROCRASTINATION

Time is your number one ally—or your number one enemy.

Consider the cost of procrastination, for example. Let's say you invest $458.33 per month. That's a total of $5,500 a year, the amount someone under the age of 50 can currently to contribute to an IRA each year. Let's also assume a 10 percent rate of return—a bit high, given recent markets, but a common assumption not long ago. Your target retirement age is 65. If you start at age 35, you will have accumulated $952,868. If you wait until you are 37, just two years later, you will be investing only $11,000 less. Not a big deal, right? The math shows otherwise: Your total at retirement will be $777,327. That's a difference of almost $176,000.

Now, if you divide that by the number of days in two years, the cost of procrastination is $240 per day. That's the decision that you are making. Take advantage of time and the power of compounding!

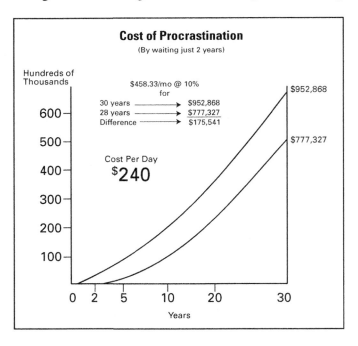

This is a hypothetical example and is not representative of any specific situation. Your results will vary. The hypothetical rates of return used do not reflect the deduction of fees and charges inherent to investing.

EXAMPLE 1: EARLY START

Let's say you graduated from college and started making the maximum contribution to an IRA ($5,500/year or $458.33/mo), starting at age 23 and continuing for 13 years, through age 34. You put in $71,500 in that period and never invest another cent. At an assumed rate of return of 10%, the value of those accounts after that period of time would be over $142,000 (see chart on next page).

EXAMPLE 2: DELAYED START

Now, suppose you instead waited until age 35 to start investing that way. Perhaps you first wanted to pay off student loans, or you just wanted to buy some expensive toys as a reward for your hard work. You decide it's now time to save for retirement, so you faithfully invest $5,500 a year until age 62.

How do those two portfolios compare at age 62? In the first scenario, you contribute for 13 years and stop. You only invest $71,500, but your portfolio totals over $2,000,000. In the second scenario, you contribute for 28 years, investing $154,000—more than twice as much—but your portfolio totals only $777,000. Let both of those sums compound for an additional five years at 10% and values are $3.29M versus $1.25M.

"EARLY" START		AGE	"DELAYED" START	
	$ 5,500	23	$	0
	$ 5,500	24	$	0
	$ 5,500	25	$	0
	$ 5,500	23	$	0
	$ 5,500	26	$	0
	$ 5,500	27	$	0
	$ 5,500	28	$	0
	$ 5,500	29	$	0
	$ 5,500	30	$	0
	$ 5,500	31	$	0
	$ 5,500	32	$	0
	$ 5,500	33	$	0
Value at age 34 $ 142,082 ($458.33/mo for 13 years at 10% compounded)	$ 5,500	34	$	0
	$ 0	35	$	5,500
	$ 0	36	$	5,500
	$ 0	37	$	5,500
	$ 0	38	$	5,500
	$ 0	39	$	5,500
	$ 0	40	$	5,500
	$ 0	41	$	5,500
	$ 0	42	$	5,500
	$ 0	43	$	5,500
	$ 0	44	$	5,500
	$ 0	45	$	5,500
	$ 0	46	$	5,500
	$ 0	47	$	5,500
	$ 0	48	$	5,500
	$ 0	49	$	5,500
	$ 0	50	$	5,500
	$ 0	51	$	5,500
	$ 0	52	$	5,500
	$ 0	53	$	5,500
	$ 0	54	$	5,500
	$ 0	55	$	5,500
	$ 0	56	$	5,500
	$ 0	57	$	5,500
	$ 0	58	$	5,500
	$ 0	59	$	5,500
	$ 0	60	$	5,500
	$ 0	61	$	5,500
	$ 0	62	$	5,500
Total Invested	$ 71,500		$	154,000
Value at Age 62*	$ 2,048,822		# $	777,328
Value at Age 67**	$ 3,298,603		## $	1,251,498

*	$ 142,082	invested for 28 yrs at 10% compounding
**	$ 2,048,822	invested for 5 yrs at 10% compounding
#	$ 458.33/mo	invested for 28 yrs at 10% compounding
##	$ 777,328	invested for 5 yrs at 10% compounding

These examples really demonstrate the power of compounding and why time is your biggest ally—or your greatest enemy. A lesson to consider: "Invest early, often, and as much as you are able."

PLAYING THE BACK NINE

You might think of life as like a golf course: You have the front nine and the back nine. Some advisors in the financial services industry focus on helping people accumulate money. That is, they're on the front nine. But a huge question is how do you get that money out, with respect to tax efficiency. That's critical. This points to the importance of working with a professional who understands distribution planning.

When most people retire, one of their major assets is a retirement plan—an IRA, a 401(k), or another in the alphabet soup of such plans. Their employer may have contributed a matching amount. The issue is how to withdraw that money efficiently in retirement to maintain one's standard of living.

An important concept here is what is known among many financial professionals as a "bucket strategy." According to one distribution strategy, you need three primary categories, or buckets, of money when you retire. You need to have 1) taxable, 2) tax-deferred, and 3) tax-free money, and you need to develop a strategy for taking the money out based on circumstances that range from personal ones to the economic and political forces that drive interest rates and taxation.

While it is fresh in our minds, lets go back and look at our "Early" Start, "Delayed" Start graphic of individuals who maximized their savings into an IRA during the years they invested. And let's say that the individual who invested $71,500 early in their life decided to make those contributions as a Roth—meaning that they paid taxes on those contributions instead of taking a tax deduction, if eligible. In other words, they had a choice to "save" income taxes on $71,500.

Over that 13-year period in the 25% tax bracket, they would have saved almost $18,000 in tax. But because they decided to elect Roth, the entire account will be free from tax. At age 67, that is more than $3.29M in a tax-free asset. Let's compare that to the individual who started late and invested a total of $154,000. If they have elected to treat the contribution as a deductible IRA, they would have saved the tax on $154,000. At a 25% tax rate, that would save them more than $38,000. Additionally, they would have deferred paying any tax on gains year after year. But here is the catch—the account has no "basis." In other words, the entire balance of the account is taxable. So what they have done is traded tax savings on $154,000 and earnings to then have an account at age 67 of more than $1.25M with a significant tax load (at 25% that would be more than $312,000—meaning their account really only has a value of about $938,000). And the fact of the matter is that they don't even know what the tax rate will be—it's like having an adjustable rate "mortgage" on a retirement account. And don't think you'll be able to just let it ride. The government was patient all these years and now they want to tax that money. How will they get it? Through a three-letter acronym—RMD. Yes, the often-dreaded required minimum distribution. It starts at age 70½, and the percentage of required withdrawal grows so that late in life the required distributions will likely outpace the growth, thereby possibly depleting the account. And don't worry if you don't get to spend it all, your heirs will get the ability to square up with the government upon your passing through another little tax called "Income with Respect to Decedent."

It's easy to help someone accumulate money. There's not a whole lot to that other than saving and investing. That's where the vast majority of the financial services industry spends its time. I compliment many people for how well they have played the front nine—

and now, I ask them: What is your plan for the back nine? And who's going to help you?

I will be discussing tax strategies in greater detail in Part Two and income planning in Part Three.

MAKING THE MOST OF THE MARKET

After the 2007–08 downturn, a lot of people got out at the bottom and waited too long to get back in. They missed the recovery.

Since the market bottomed in 2009, I have watched the recovery with awe as the market defied predictions that it was due for a major correction. The best advice that I can provide to my clients is to implement strategies with the goal to take advantage of rising markets but also protect them in the event of a surprise downturn.

The market is something of an emotional beast. It has its scientific side, but it does not have to act by any particular set of rules. It is a truly free market—and it is hard to predict. There's one thing I can tell you with certainty about what the market will do on any given day, week, month or year: It will either go up, or it will go down, or it will stay the same.

Nobody knows what's going to happen in the near term. Through the years, we will have some violent downturns in the market, and we will have some exuberant rises. I do believe in the long-term growth of the economy.

The concept of "dollar cost averaging" is a wonderful strategy during the accumulation phase to take a lot of the emotion away from investing. As you continue to regularly invest, the market rises

51

and falls and rises anew. When it's down, you are buying your shares at a bargain. The effect over time is a significant reduction in your cost per share, even in a market that has only gone sideways.

You can think of a downturn as the market holding a sale. Back in 2008–09, when the Dow was down in the 6000s, stocks essentially were on sale. It seems Americans will buy anything on sale except stocks. When it comes to investing, so many people rush to buy after the price rises. What's up with that?

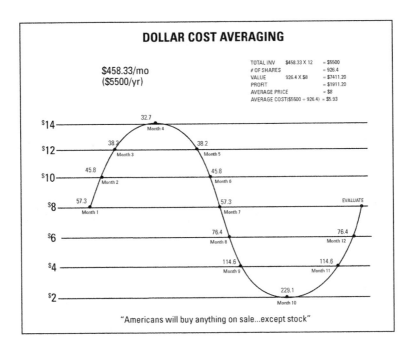

DOLLAR COST AVERAGING

$458.33/mo
($5500/yr)

TOTAL INV	$458.33 X 12	= $5500
# OF SHARES		= 926.4
VALUE	926.4 X $8	= $7411.20
PROFIT		= $1911.20
AVERAGE PRICE		= $8
AVERAGE COST($5500 ÷ 926.4)		= $5.93

"Americans will buy anything on sale...except stock"

Many studies have been done on the consequences of investor behavior. A number of tools will show you the difference in the rate of return if you missed the best day on the market, or the best week, or the best 30 days.

This chart shows that by missing the 15 best single days in the market, the growth of $1,000 from 1970 to 2013 would grow to $29,378 instead of $77,804 if you stayed fully invested.

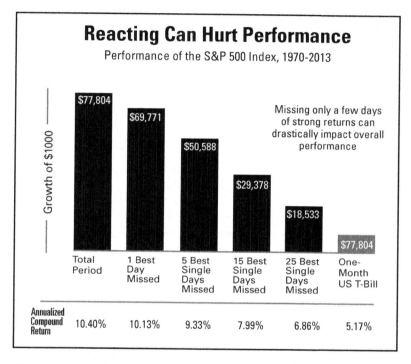

Reacting Can Hurt Performance

Performance of the S&P 500 Index, 1970-2013

Growth of $1000

$77,804

$69,771

$50,588

Missing only a few days of strong returns can drastically impact overall performance

$29,378

$18,533

$77,804

	Total Period	1 Best Day Missed	5 Best Single Days Missed	15 Best Single Days Missed	25 Best Single Days Missed	One-Month US T-Bill
Annualized Compound Return	10.40%	10.13%	9.33%	7.99%	6.86%	5.17%

In US dollars, indices are not available for direct investment. Their performance does not reflect the expenses associated with the management of an actual portfolio. Past performance is not a guarantee of future resuts. Performance data for January 1970 - August 2008 provided by CRSP, performance data for September 2008 - December 2013 provided by Bloomberg. S&P data provided by Standard & Poor's Index Service Group. US bonds and bills data © Stocks, Bonds, Bills, and Inflation Yearbook™, Ibbotson Associates, Chicago (annually updated work by Roger G. Ibbotson and Rex A Sinquefield).

These examples all point to a single concept: **Stay invested**. You have to stay invested because the market goes up, it goes down, and (historically) it goes back up. That has been true for decades. Staying fully invested is how you achieve financial wealth, not by trying to time the market. Not by trying to get in and out. Not by trying to find some hot tip.

This chart shows that markets have rewarded patient and disciplined investors, turning $1 invested in 1970 into $43 by 2013

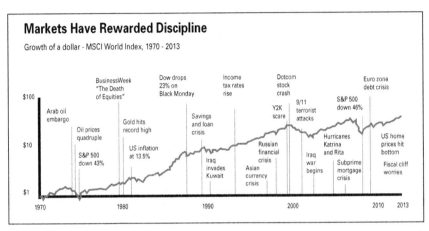

Markets Have Rewarded Discipline

Growth of a dollar - MSCI World Index, 1970 - 2013

Past performance is no guarantee of future results. MSCI data © MSCI 2013, all rights reserved. Indices are not available for direct investment, therefore, their performance does not reflect the expenses associated with the management of an actual portfolio.

Again: Time is your ally. If you spend your entire working career saving and investing, you can very well become a millionaire. We're getting to the point now—and I hope most Americans realize this—that if you are not a millionaire, it will be hard to retire with the standard of living you would like to have.

Not only is it necessary to be a millionaire, but it is also achievable.

The following chart shows how compound interest can get you pretty far. In fact, Business Insider calculated - based on your current age and a 6% return rate - how much you need to be saving per month in order to reach $1 million by age 65.

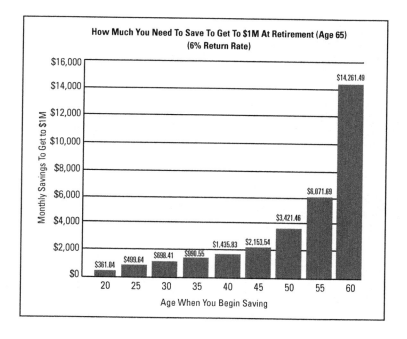

LUMP SUM INVESTMENTS COMPOUNDING ANNUALLY

YR	1%	2%	3%	4%	5%	6%	7%	8%	9%	10%
1	1.01	1.02	1.03	1.04	1.05	1.06	1.07	1.08	1.09	1.10
2	1.02	1.04	1.06	1.06	1.10	1.12	1.14	1.17	1.19	1.21
3	1.03	1.06	1.09	1.12	1.16	1.19	1.23	1.26	1.30	1.33
4	1.04	1.08	1.13	1.17	1.22	1.26	1.31	1.36	1.41	1.46
5	1.05	1.10	1.16	1.22	1.28	1.34	1.40	1.47	1.54	1.61
6	1.06	1.13	1.19	1.27	1.34	1.42	1.50	1.59	1.68	1.77
7	1.07	1.15	1.23	1.32	1.41	1.50	1.61	1.71	1.83	1.95
8	1.08	1.17	1.27	1.37	1.48	1.59	1.72	1.85	1.99	2.14
9	1.09	1.20	1.30	1.42	1.55	1.69	1.84	2.00	2.17	2.36
10	1.10	1.22	1.34	1.48	1.63	1.79	1.97	2.16	2.37	2.59
11	1.12	1.24	1.38	1.54	1.71	1.90	2.10	2.33	2.58	2.85
12	1.13	1.27	1.43	1.60	1.80	2.01	2.25	2.52	2.81	3.14
13	1.14	1.29	1.47	1.67	1.89	2.13	2.41	2.72	3.07	3.45
14	1.15	1.32	1.51	1.73	1.98	2.26	2.58	2.94	3.34	3.80
15	1.16	1.35	1.56	1.80	2.08	2.40	2.76	3.17	3.64	4.18
16	1.17	1.37	1.60	1.87	2.18	2.54	2.95	3.43	3.97	4.59
17	1.18	1.40	1.65	1.95	2.29	2.69	3.16	3.70	4.33	5.05
18	1.20	1.43	1.70	2.03	2.41	2.85	3.38	4.00	4.72	5.56
19	1.21	1.46	1.75	2.11	2.53	3.03	3.62	4.32	5.14	6.12
20	1.22	1.49	1.81	2.19	2.65	3.21	3.87	4.66	5.60	6.73
21	1.23	1.52	1.86	2.28	2.79	3.40	4.14	5.03	6.11	7.40
22	1.24	1.55	1.92	2.37	2.93	3.60	4.43	5.44	6.66	8.14
23	1.26	1.58	1.97	2.46	3.07	3.82	4.74	5.87	7.26	8.95
24	1.27	1.61	2.03	2.56	3.23	4.05	5.07	6.34	7.91	9.85
25	1.28	1.64	2.09	2.67	3.39	4.29	5.43	6.85	8.62	10.83
26	1.30	1.67	2.16	2.77	3.56	4.55	5.81	7.40	9.40	11.92
27	1.31	1.71	2.22	2.88	3.73	4.82	6.21	7.99	10.25	13.11
28	1.32	1.74	2.29	3.00	3.92	5.11	6.65	8.63	11.17	14.42
29	1.33	1.78	2.36	3.12	4.12	5.42	7.11	9.32	12.17	15.86
30	1.35	1.81	2.43	3.24	4.32	5.74	7.61	10.06	13.27	17.45

This table represents the hypothetical growth of $1 at varying compounding rates and time periods. You can use this table as a quick reference to view the potential impact of compounding on a hypothetical investment without the deduction of any fees or expenses. For example, to determine the ultimate value of a $1,000 lump sum invested at 8% for 30 years, refer to the 8% column and line 30 (30 years). The factor is 10.06 which, multiplied by $1,000, equals approximately $10,060. If the rate of growth was increased to 10% annually, the result would be $17,450 ($1,000 x 17.45).

MONTHLY INVESTMENTS COMPOUNDING ANNUALLY

YR	1%	2%	3%	4%	5%	6%	7%	8%	9%	10%
1	12	12	12	12	12	12	12	13	13	13
2	24	25	25	25	25	26	26	26	26	27
3	37	37	38	38	39	39	40	41	41	42
4	49	50	51	52	53	54	55	56	58	59
5	62	63	65	66	68	70	72	73	75	77
6	74	77	79	81	84	86	89	92	95	98
7	87	90	93	97	100	104	108	112	116	120
8	100	104	108	113	118	123	128	133	139	145
9	113	118	124	130	136	142	149	156	164	172
10	126	133	140	147	155	163	172	181	191	201
11	140	148	156	165	175	185	197	208	221	234
12	153	163	173	184	196	209	223	237	253	270
13	167	178	190	204	218	234	251	269	289	310
14	180	194	208	224	242	260	281	303	327	354
15	194	210	227	245	266	288	313	340	369	402
16	208	226	246	268	292	318	347	379	415	454
17	222	243	265	290	318	349	384	422	465	513
18	237	260	286	314	347	383	423	469	519	576
19	251	277	306	339	376	418	465	519	579	647
20	266	295	328	365	407	456	510	573	643	724
21	280	313	350	392	440	495	559	631	714	809
22	295	331	372	420	474	537	610	694	791	903
23	310	350	396	449	511	582	665	762	875	1005
24	325	369	420	479	548	629	724	835	966	1119
25	341	389	445	511	588	680	787	915	1065	1243
26	356	408	470	543	630	733	855	1001	1174	1380
27	372	429	496	577	674	789	927	1093	1292	1531
28	388	449	524	613	720	849	1005	1193	1421	1696
29	404	471	551	649	768	912	1087	1301	1561	1879
30	420	492	580	688	819	979	1176	1418	1714	2079

This table represents the hypothetical growth of $1 at varying compounding rates and time periods. You can use this table as a quick reference to view the potential impact of compounding on a hypothetical investment without the deduction of any fees or expenses. For example, to determine the ultimate value of a $458.33 monthly investment at 8% for 30 years, refer to the 8% column and line 30 (30 years). The factor is 1418 which, multiplied by $458.33, equals approximately $649,912. If the rate of growth was increased to 10% annually, the result would be $952,868 ($458.33 x 2079).

CHAPTER 4

PAY YOURSELF FIRST

S oon after I was commissioned in the army, I was introduced to a company whose focus was financial planning for military professionals. I began to pay myself first and started investing with my second paycheck in the army. I started making contributions to an overall financial plan.

I noticed that most of the representatives of the financial planning company were retired military officers, and I recall thinking that I could see myself doing planning, too, when I retired someday.

I was stationed in Berlin, and I remember sitting at the Officers' Club one day when I had been in Germany about two years. My peers at the table were complaining that they were broke at (or even before) the end of each month. Every one of them made the same amount of money that I did and lived basically the same lifestyle, but they had nothing to show for it.

I, too, was out of money at the end of each month, but the difference was that at the beginning of each month I'd consistently put money into my financial plan. I had been learning to pay myself first. I realized that I was the only one at that table who was living within his means; no one in the military gives orders to make you save, you have to set it up on your own.

It was in Berlin that I met Theresa, a Department of Defense schoolteacher. We married in 1990, and I decided to conclude my service at the end of my obligation. I left the army in 1991. An international financial planning company gave me an opportunity at Fort Leonard Wood, Missouri. There, I had the opportunity to help young officers just as I once had been helped. It was my focus and my passion to help young officers to get started on the right path financially. I had seen how getting started early had helped me. Time was on my side, and it was on theirs, too.

I tell my clients the same thing today. In fact, I believe it so strongly that my license plate says, "Pay yourself first." It's a concept that I was taught at the beginning of my investing years. Before spending on lifestyle, paying bills, and other obligations, you need to put yourself at the top of your list. By paying yourself first, I mean setting aside money for your future. Take a position of priority on your own payroll, before all those to whom you dole out the dollars: the mortgage company, the utilities, the tax collector, and the rest. Decide on the percentage that your financial plan needs, based on your goals, and then build your lifestyle around that. And remember, your financial plan is more than investments. It includes savings and insurance—protecting against short- and long-term risks that could derail your plan.

In no way does "pay yourself first" mean you should be less generous to others. Generosity comes back to you, so as you give to others, you too benefit. We should share our treasures, including our time and our talents. Most people are very giving in nature: They contribute financially, or tithe, or they donate their time. Maybe it's a Saturday or Sunday each month or quarter that they contribute to a cause that they care about—a local place of worship, perhaps, or a homeless shelter or soup kitchen. If you have a particular skill set or talent—you're a great bookkeeper, or carpenter, or attorney—you can help others. These are all ways that we can give back. Each of us in our own way can find the right balance in reaching out.

Then, ask yourself how you rate on your own payroll. You should be at the top. Are you saving and investing for your future? You deserve to be at the top of your payroll before mortgages and any of the toys or other things that you spend money on. Your retirement depends on it. "Pay yourself first" is my core belief for financial success. It is not selfish. It is selfless. The more you can save and invest and grow your resources, the more capacity you will have to give back.

The concept of paying yourself first means that all the other uses for your money come afterward, including giving to the government in taxes. I would never want anyone to think that I was not a proponent of paying all the legally required taxes, I am. But I also know that some people pay more than the legally required taxes and do not know that they are doing so. They are giving to the government more than it actually requires of them.

There are perfectly legitimate ways to use the tax code to your advantage—and you might consider that hiring a specialist to help you uncover those savings is one good way to find the dollars to pay yourself first.

BUDGET SUCCESS FUNDAMENTALS

So far so good—but how do you set this up? You need to develop a budget. You need to establish priorities. You're the only person who's going to take care of you—and you can do so through the power of budgeting, determining what you want to spend on the present you and how much on the future you.

Let's take a closer look at how you can budget effectively. This is a service that we provide for our clients. No matter your age, a good budget will deal with some basic considerations:

- What is your gross income monthly? (for you and your partner, if applicable)
- What deductions come out of your pay? (federal income taxes, state and local taxes, Medicare, Social Security)
- How much are you going to be saving for your future? (in a 401(k) for retirement, for a home, a car, college, and other goals)
- How much do you pay as your portion of employment benefits? (Health, dental, vision, FSA, disability insurance, etc.)
- What will you be paying in income taxes? (withholding considerations)

After determining how much those things are going to cost, you get to a net number. This is your take-home pay. If the deductions include an employer-sponsored retirement plan, then you have already paid yourself first—at least to some extent. If not, then you need to do so with an investment plan.

Then, what are some of the things you will need? Let's talk about the basics.

You're going to need a place to live, and that means you will be paying rent or a mortgage. One of the things that I like to point out to people is that when you buy a home, it's more than the principal, interest, taxes, and insurance. You need to consider utilities and maintenance and other costs of home ownership that you might not have as a renter. When something breaks in your home, it is your responsibility; you cannot simply call the landlord. In addition to having a personal emergency fund, do you have an emergency fund for your home? Also, out of pride, people tend to spend more on a home they own. So it's not an apple-to-apple comparison when considering whether to rent or buy. You need to factor in a lot of considerations.

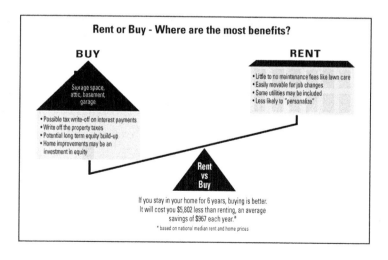

Then we get down to line items, such as groceries and transportation costs and lifestyle expenses. Will you shop at the supermarket, or will you mostly be dining out? Will you take public transportation or buy a car? What kind of a car? What about insurance and parking costs? Lifestyle expenses include cell phone and Internet and cable, recreation, and vacations and trips. You need to always examine the balance between fixed and variable expenses—the "must haves" and the "nice to haves."

You need to take a hard look at where the money goes and prioritize. The early years can be tough. Sometimes young people leave the nest and expect to just step into the same lifestyle they enjoyed growing up. They may need a reminder of the meager times their parents went through at their age, working hard and saving to gradually increase their standard of living. The attitude of "I deserve it now" is a "keeping up with the Joneses" mentality.

There are so many aspects to budgeting and so many considerations—but it is not optional. After paying yourself first, you must know where the rest of your money is going.

THE DEBT TRAP

It's important to understand the difference in types of debt. Some is constructive and some is destructive. An example of constructive debt is a home mortgage. Rarely can people save enough money to pay cash for a home, and it's perhaps unrealistic to expect to do so. Such debt traditionally has been constructive, allowing homeowners to both put a roof over their heads and invest in real estate that they expected to increase in value. By contrast, destructive debt is the kind that drains assets through interest charges, such as the onerous charges some people pay on multiple consumer credit cards.

You need to be cautious that your overall debt to income ratio is in check. Even though a lender may be comfortable with a 40 percent income to debt ratio, are you? Lenders often apply rules of thumb, but the recent credit crisis has called into question the methods by which credit is extended and to whom.

Mortgage companies are among the best when it comes to scrutinizing your ability to pay for a home. The last thing they want to be is a landlord. They want you to be successful at paying your mortgage and owning your home. They look closely at your other obligations and the impact the mortgage would have on you. When they look at the credit lines on your cards, they assume you will have maxed them out and be paying only the minimums. That is a good, conservative approach.

Other lenders may not be so cautious. Be wary of those who are willing to extend credit without making you jump through a few hoops. They likely are not looking at the whole picture. The beauty of having a budget is that you will know whether the new obligation will fit. The final approval lies with you.

Consumer debt can be a vicious cycle. Interest rates are low right now for borrowing. I believe it would not be a stretch to say that the average American household has about $10,000 in credit card debt. At 12 percent, that's $1,200 a year in interest, or $100 a month. What if you were to invest that $100 a month instead of giving it to the credit card company?

Credit card companies often require that you pay only 1½ to 3 percent of the balance each month. If you pay only 1½ percent of $10,000, that's only $150 a month. You may never escape, or it will take you a phenomenally long time. Laws have been passed that compel creditors to provide that information. You may have noticed those changes on your credit card statements. For example, if you pay only the minimum 1.5 percent on $35,696, which is $535, it will take you 36 years to pay off the debt. If you "double" the minimum payment, to $1,079 the debt is gone in three years. After that, consider the impact of saving or investing $1,079 for 33 years (use the compound interest tables found on page 56-57 for more).

Minimum payment due:	$535.00
New balance:	$35,696.39
Payment due date:	08/10/14

Late Payment Warning: If we do not receive your minimum payment by the date listed above, you may have to pay a late fee of up to $35 and your APRs may be increased up to the variable Penalty APR of 29.99%.

Minimum Payment Warning: If you make only the minimum payment each period, you will pay more in interest and it will take longer to pay off your balance. For example:

If you make no additional charges using this card and each month you pay...	You will pay off the balance shown on this statement in about...	And you will end up paying an estimated total of...
Only the minimum payment	36 years	$71,768
$1,079	3 year(s)	$38,837 (Savings = $32,931)

If you have a lot of credit card debt, it's an indication that you have failed in your budgeting exercise. Typically, it means you did not have the financial resources to cover certain expenses. In other words, you overspent. Perhaps you ran into an emergency. You don't know when the washer or dryer will break down, your car's transmission will fail, or your kid will break an arm and need to go to the emergency room.

Maybe you lost your job. But a good budget will build up emergency savings to sustain you in such situations. You must be diligent in contributing to that fund and not divert the money to other uses even after your emergency savings bucket is full. That way if you ever face a true emergency and deplete your emergency savings, you will have a line item in your budget to replenish it. This will help you avoid the debt trap.

I'm not saying that your financial decisions always have to make 100 percent financial sense. For example, you may wonder whether you should pay off your home mortgage. I could demonstrate to you that in many cases carrying a mortgage makes mathematical sense due to the interest deduction on taxation and how you could otherwise use that money. But at the end of the day, if the mortgage causes you sleepless nights, then pay it off. The math is a guide, not a rule.

It's your financial plan. It's about what's important to you. Your budget has to reflect how you want to live your life, and it has to be done with care and wisdom and good advice.

CHAPTER 5

TIME, NOT TIMING

Oftentimes, I'll ask people, "When is the best time to have planted a shade tree?" I get a variety of answers, but many people say 20 years ago or 30 years ago. And I'll say, "That's probably right. When is the next best time to plant a shade tree?" And the answer is today.

In other words, we have whatever time we have left. This is not about going back and beating yourself up. Some people get to a point where they feel hopeless. They tell themselves they should have saved but didn't do it, and therefore it's too late. Not so: It's never too late to start.

"Coulda, woulda, shoulda" is no way to go through life. Look instead to the future, and do what you can right now to make things better. We have to use whatever time we have left as powerfully as we can. People come up with a lot of excuses as to why they can't get started or why they don't want to do this or that. They are putting obstacles in their own path.

Think of it like this: If you drive to work, there will be many red lights along the way. There will be many yellows. You may face traffic jams and detours. Would you wait until all of the lights were green before you pulled out of the driveway? Of course not. You would begin your commute and deal with each of the lights as you came upon it.

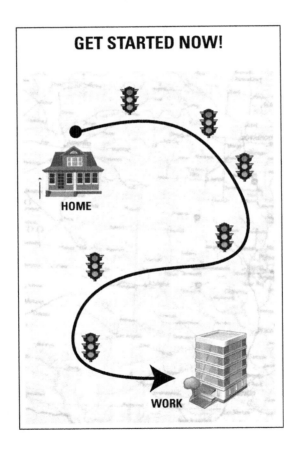

That is how you need to view your financial plan. Life is not a straight line, nor is it an exponential curve. Life is full of ups and

downs. Many of them are pleasant. You get a college education. You get married and have a baby. You buy a home. You put your children through college. Some are unpleasant: the death of a loved one, or a divorce, or the loss of a job. You certainly shouldn't wait until all your lights are green before heading out on the trip. You can enjoy the ride and deal with life's issues if and when they come to you.

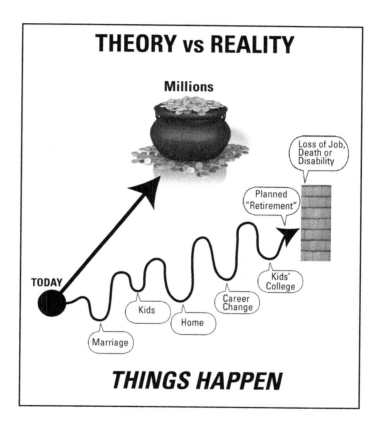

So plant the shade tree now if you haven't planted it already. That sapling soon will give you a little shade and then more and more—and the generation ahead will enjoy its spreading boughs. And if you've already planted that tree, water and fertilize.

It's often said that most people spend more time planning a family vacation than they spend planning their financial future. That's pretty easy to say since most people don't spend any time at all planning their financial future. Why is that? Well, a vacation is fun. When you plan one, you anticipate the reward. You are eager to figure out how you will get there, what you will do there, where you will get the money. Financial planning, by contrast, seems a chore—and yet, essentially, retirement is the longest vacation you will ever be on. You need to figure out how to get there, what you will do there—and where you will get the money.

There seems to be some mystery associated with financial planning. Remember: Financial planning is not wealth management. I think that's the hang-up for a lot of people. They think that financial planning is picking stocks. As we have seen, it entails far more than that.

NOT ABOUT TIMING THE MARKET

I have discussed the nuances of time in a number of ways in these pages—the quality of time, the value of time, the time it takes for a financial plan to work effectively. Perhaps you also thought I was going to talk about timing the market. Let me be clear: You can't do that.

The average stock picker or professional mutual fund manager is wrong about seven out of ten times. And if you think you are better than that, then you are either lucky or you are in the wrong profession. A baseball player who has a .300 average or a .350 average is considered an excellent hitter. The same is true in stock picking.

In what I call the do-it-yourselfer world, all you ever hear about is everyone's winners. Nobody ever tells you about the losers. Whether they are talking about stock picks or real estate, all that anybody seems to ever really remember is whatever did well. They're not bashful when they talk about it. But just ask them, "How many losers did you pick? What did that do to your portfolio?" Silence.

It is virtually impossible to time the market, and part of the reason, again, is that the market has a technical side and an emotional side. There is a definite mathematical element to it, without a doubt. A whole sector of our industry is dedicated to charts and graphs and trends and breakout points. For some people, it's a passion.

The market, however, is an auction. Whenever you have an auction, you are dealing with emotion, and not everybody is playing by the same rules. If everybody was a technician and played strictly by the technical aspects of the market, things would be more predictable. But it only takes a few flies in the ointment to screw things up. It could be internal or external forces. It could be the decisions made by the players in the market or within a company, or it could be a foreign crisis or industry change that impacts a company's value and stock price.

Because the market is an auction, with an emotional element of it, trying to time it is just not a good strategy. Perhaps you feel you can do as the gurus do. You have your favorite financial wizard out there and you'll just watch and see what he or she does and then copycat. It won't work. First, you have a different financial plan and needs. And even if that guru's decisions were good for you, it would be too late to follow suit. By the time you knew about what was going on and invested accordingly, the gurus and all their followers would have already made their plays. You would be getting in at the wrong time.

We tell our clients to stop watching the financial "news" networks and the 24-hour news flow about the financial world. I think it's a waste of time, and viewers get the wrong impressions. The commentators know nothing about your particular situation—your values, goals, and resources.

I once had the opportunity to meet Peter Lynch, the venerable manager of the Fidelity Magellan Fund, when he spoke at a conference. You may recall that during the tech boom of the '90s, day trading was popular. Lynch's take on day trading was that people would be better off going to a casino—the results are about the same, and there's a lot less paperwork.

BEST USE OF YOUR TIME

I have many clients who are professionals. Some are very detail oriented and are prone to suffer from what I call paralysis by analysis. They feel the need to crank out every possible combination and permutation. If financial planning were pure science, I could be replaced by a computer program. But no computer program can understand the art of financial planning. It takes finesse to help someone align their most deeply held values with their most important goals.

I try to help my clients who are experts in their own fields understand that delegating financial matters does not suggest they are not smart. It's just suggesting that maybe there's a better use of their time.

I can't remember the last time I mowed a lawn, although I know I'm pretty good at it. Mowing lawns is how I earned my first dollars when I was a boy. But now I hire a lawn service—not because I'm incapable but because lawn care is not the best use of my time. I could spend hours researching fertilizers and pruning techniques. Instead, I have decided that the best use of my time is in two places. One is with my family, enjoying them. And the other is with my clients, helping them. I don't have a lot of time in between. So I delegate. I outsource. That way I can focus on what is important to me.

As part of values-based financial planning, I help people weigh the value of delegating by walking them through a "quality of life" exercise. It's a worksheet on which they list various activities and, for each, decide whether it could be delegated, how much time they would like to spend on the activity each week, three ways they could improve that aspect of their life, and the impact of those improvements.

THE ART OF DELEGATION

What Could I Delegate?	How Many Hours Would I Save Each Week?	What Could I Choose To Do With "The Gift Of Time"?	What Impact Would This Have On My Life, or The Lives of Others?

Now, while I suppose you could delegate date nights with your spouse, I don't recommend that. That's something for you to keep to yourself. However, you very likely would delegate other things in your life that would free you up for even more date nights.

Though I lost Theresa at such a young age, I don't feel as though we denied ourselves anything. We were a close family. We did a lot of things. And for those times together, I'm grateful. Had we focused only on keeping our noses to the grindstone, I'd be full of regrets.

That's why I encourage my clients to get out and enjoy themselves. Life is precious. We might think we have years left for all we want to do, but none of us really knows. Each day is a gift to be used well.

A BEST-IN-CLASS TEAM

Sometimes, people drive themselves hard out of fear of the unknown. They don't know whether they'll have enough for their families, and so they just keep at it, at all costs. That underscores the need for financial planning—so that they do know. For most people, financial planning is a good thing to delegate.

A professional can help you find the right balance. You will discover how much you need to save, and how often, to reach a particular goal. Advisors can help with direction and using your resources most efficiently. You may find that you have more time than you thought for your family and the other important things in life.

Even if you enjoy crunching numbers, that's only the science side. You also need the art. A good financial planner can help with both. The world has certainly not become less complex. We are living longer, and we are more active. As we gain opportunities to do more things, we need more resources. And the more ingredients in a recipe, the better the chef must be. It takes experience to know the right way to mix, blend, and bake.

There was a time, now gone, when a solo practitioner could probably handle the complexity of a financial plan. If you're the jack of all trades, you tend to be the master of none. The best teams have a central financial planner who delegates specific tasks to experts in their respective fields.

A financial planner is like an orchestra conductor. Can a conductor play an instrument? Absolutely. Can he play it well? I would imagine so. But if he were to go out and sit in the orchestra, would he be the best musician there? No. And nobody would expect that. The conductor is supposed to be the one who sees the big picture. He knows how the piece should sound and how each section and player and instrument will contribute to it. He is the master of connections, and he brings together the best musicians he can assemble to create a masterpiece of exquisite timing.

Likewise, the role of financial planners should be to assemble a best-in-class team. They don't need to know every bit of the tax code and tax law, but they had better know somebody who does. You need a financial planner whom you can trust to know the right steps, who can readily identify the issues and lay out the options. By yourself, you can't possibly process everything. No individual has that breadth of expertise.

A lot of people hang out a shingle and call themselves financial planners or advisors. The title is loosely used, and the industry needs to work on clarifying it. A true financial planner rallies a team and helps you to consider the wide range of quality-of-life issues—not just how to grow your portfolio.

It's time, not timing, that is important. Think, always, about what matters in life. That's the premise of our business. Our tagline is not: "Hunker down over those spreadsheets." It is this: "Live Your Ideal Life." That's what it's all about. When you understand that, you understand the true value of time.

CHAPTER 6

DESTINATION: "RETIREMENT"

" I think the wall's going to come down," Theresa told me as we parted in Berlin for several days in November 1989. She was heading to a weekend teachers' retreat in West Germany, where they were doing a literary tour of the Grimm Brothers' fairy tales. I was on a training operation in an area flanking the Berlin Wall—which, in that section, was actually a fence. The East Germans had guard posts where they could peer in and watch us conduct our training missions.

There had been a lot of unrest in East Germany, but it seemed preposterous to me that the wall could come down. "Have fun on your trip," I told her. She would be gone until Sunday night. "I'll see you Tuesday," I said—that's when the exercise was to end.

I was a scout platoon leader, an enviable position in the lieutenant world. The most coveted position was to be a specialty platoon leader in the combat support company. I had both a scout platoon and a sniper platoon. It was the premier position to have. One must be qualified, of course, but good timing helps; There were other well-qualified lieutenants to take the platoon, but I happened to be available and eligible, and it was my time to rotate.

The training area was called Doughboy City, a mock city with buildings where we could train. My platoon was the eyes and the ears of the battalion. I would send them out on a mission, they would report to me, and I would report to the battalion commander.

My platoon was out all night, and at about 6 a.m. I was standing at the hood of my battalion commander's Humvee, debriefing him on the night's training operations. The sun was just starting to come up. Down the road, a Mercedes came screaming into the operational area.

The district mayor got out of the car and approached the battalion commander. "How can you be training for war on such a glorious day?" he asked.

"What the hell are you talking about?" We wondered if he had just stumbled out of a bar.

"The wall has fallen!" The unthinkable had happened. It was true. While we were on the training exercise all night, the wall had fallen.

The inevitable had happened. The wall was bound to come down one day, and though we had kept a close watch on matters, the big event still felt as if it had come by surprise. I think about that night sometimes as I work today with people on the brink of retirement. They knew that the day would be coming. Many of them have planned carefully. But they didn't know what it would be like until they got there.

A REALISTIC 'PLAYCHECK'

I don't have very many rules, but there is one that I really like: You cannot simply list "retirement" as a goal. You cannot say that a "mortgage-free home" is a goal. Instead, what I want to know is what that phase of life means to you. What does retirement represent for you?

The thought of "retirement" should spark something within you. You should be anticipating something worthwhile. For many individuals, it's not the end. It's the beginning of the next chapter in their lives.

I get some wonderful responses to my question. "It's when my paycheck is now a play check," one client told me. This paints a picture of plans to pursue a world of opportunity, no longer working for money but rather letting the money work for him. He has big plans for the years ahead.

I believe that an active lifestyle leads to a longer life. Being engaged in life promotes longevity, as medical studies have indicated. I have seen the evidence in my own practice, and I believe that proper financial planning will position people to continue leading active lives. Perhaps the Surgeon General should publish another notice: "Proper financial planning leads to long life."

When the Social Security system was developed, people didn't live long into retirement. Social Security was meant to bridge a three- to five-year gap before death. The system wasn't a bad idea for the time, but it was based on a set of assumptions that no longer are true. People are living far longer today than anybody anticipated at that time.

That's why we need more financial planners who know how to play the back nine. In a society in which baby boomers are retiring in droves, only a few percent of the planners specialize in dealing with the issues that they face. It's important and necessary to accumulate money, of course, but once you've accomplished that, what do you do with it? How do you start putting that money to work, making sure that it will last for the rest of your life, however long that might be?

Traditional financial planning doesn't involve a lot of human interaction. It's pretty much just computer-based modeling. It doesn't include conversations about the reality of aging. We take a different approach. We help you develop a list of things you want to do and places you want to see, and we help you develop a realistic timeframe. If you tell us you want to spend $25,000 a year on major trips, I'll suggest that might be all right in your 60s and into your 70s, but will you still need that much in your 80s and beyond? Or will your trips be shorter and closer to home? Or will you be staying at home while people come to see you?

In other words, as you think about accomplishing your goals, you need to understand that some expenses come earlier and some come later. Some taper off with age. Perhaps all of your world trips will be in the first five years of retirement, followed by several years of visiting spots in the United States, then regional and local destinations. One must apply the reality of mobility to retirement planning. A lot of people don't think about that, and those are the kind of considerations that we help to bring to the surface.

Living longer means you will need more money, which means you need to start planning earlier. *The Richest Man in Babylon* (that is the title of a book, by the way) might say you should invest 10 percent of everything you make. Is that enough? It might be, if you start early in life and are consistent. But most of us would say it's probably insufficient. How can you expect to put some relatively small percentage of your pay into a financial plan and have it kick out a full salary for almost the same number of years that you were working? The math doesn't work out well.

WHEN DO YOU WANT TO KNOW?

"I just can't retire," people sometimes tell me when they come in for a consultation. They don't see how they could do without that paycheck or how they could sell their business.

"Well, how do you know you cannot retire?" I ask.

"Well, I've just got to keep working."

"So when do you want to know when you can retire? Because I bet you would be making some different choices if you knew it could happen way sooner than you thought possible."

If you are working with a specialist in retirement planning, you can get a clear picture of the possibilities. You can find out whether and when you can retire.

There are a lot of nuances to that decision. I don't make a general recommendation as to when people should apply for Social Security, because it's a very individual decision. It depends on a lot of factors. Are you a widow or widower? Are you currently married? Were you previously married? Did your divorced spouse make more money than you made? Depending upon your financial situation, perhaps you should start drawing your Social Security benefit at age 62 or defer until age 70.

An entire set of planning assumptions is based on just the Social Security consideration. And then we need to coordinate all the other sources of income that an individual has, such as a pension. A lot of pensions give you the opportunity to take out a sum of money now or take out a greater sum later.

Today's typical retirees could have up to three sources of income. They'll have Social Security; they'll have some sort of defined benefit or defined contribution plan (401(k), 403(b), pension), whether they're self-employed or not; and then they will have their private accumulated assets, which could be IRAs, personal savings, personal investments, equity and property, etc.

Another important consideration is: What is the tax treatment of all of those different distribution plans? And what impact will that have on other benefits, such as your Social Security benefits? Will they be taxed? How much of them will be taxed? How much of that has to be included in your income?

Are you taking required minimum distributions because you have to, or are you taking them because you need to? That's an important question to answer. Are you taking money out of an IRA because the government says you must do so and then subjecting that withdrawal to taxation—with a ripple effect that forces you to lower other benefits? It can become a cascading or a snowballing effect.

Retirement planning also includes determining the legacy that you wish to leave. As you approach this phase of life when your money will work for you instead of vice versa, you have three basic questions to answer. We pose those questions to all our clients: Do you want to spend more, give more, or leave more? One of those three, or a combination, is what's going to end up happening.

The list of considerations goes on and on. Maybe you know a lot of the answers, but most people wonder where to begin. Let me reassure you that you are not alone.

PART TWO

THE 6 BIG RISKS®

I t has often been said that people don't really care how much you know until they know how much you care—and I believe that is true. They also may have attitudes and preconceived notions about financial planning. I was taught by one of the founding partners of Cornerstone that it's difficult to pour tea into a full cup. And so I always ask the question, "What's on your mind?"

Financial planning, for many people, is a mysterious and complex and confusing subject. In explaining it, I often put it like this: "My job is to help protect you against THE 6 BIG RISKS®." I feel that is my role. That describes financial planning in a way people can understand. They get it.

We also ask a version of what is known as "The Dan Sullivan Question," as suggested by that author. "If we were having this conversation three years from today, what would have to have happened over the last three years, both personally and professionally, for you to feel happy about your progress?" That helps people drill down to their purpose in financial planning.

We also ask: "What is your definition of financial planning?" Most people's answers are focused on money management or wealth management. That gives us an idea of the client's perspective on the matter. We're not looking to see if they understand all about annuities or the latest financial fads. We want to see if they have been thinking about where they are in life and what needs to come first.

My crusade is to help educate the American public that financial planning is not wealth management, as the public has been conditioned to believe. Most people's relationships in the financial services industry have been with salespeople who work for a commission. I understand that, and in the early days of my career, that's what I did. I grew up in that system.

Today, my goal is to get the word out about true financial planning. I try to counteract people's conditioned response. Once they are satisfied and can see how much they have been helped, they let down their defensive shield—and they want to refer others.

In our media-driven world, information is instant and accessible. It's with us everywhere we go unless we shut it off. People are looking for ways to make complex subjects simpler and more manageable. Our practice is built on that theme. We wish to be the central source for your financial planning needs. We take an "ensemble" approach that rallies the experiences of our entire team. Each member has a specific area of expertise, generally driven by a passion for a particular subject.

You would be pleased with the conversations that take place among our team while you're not there. We get into spirited debates over the proper approach for a particular client. This is no cookie-cutter-style of financial planning. You get the talents and perspectives of a variety of experts—and that's something an ensemble can offer that you cannot get from a solo practitioner.

Together, my team and I have the fundamental role of protecting clients against THE 6 BIG RISKS®, each of which is detailed in a chapter in this section of the book.

CHAPTER 1

DYING TOO SOON

It wasn't long after I started my private practice when Theresa became ill.

It was the weekend of Martin Luther King Day in 2010. After we had spent a day on the ski slopes, Theresa said she wasn't feeling well and wanted to lie down. As she rested, the girls and I drove into town.

When we returned, I checked on Theresa. She had indigestion. "Let me just rest a few more hours," she said. "I may want to go home." By Monday evening, she'd had an ultrasound, and her gallbladder had been removed. The doctor said it appeared to be infected.

The call from the doctor's office came a couple days later. "We really want to talk with you."

When they removed her gallbladder, they had discovered a tumor, and it was cancerous. She had major surgery to have her liver resectioned. She responded well to chemotherapy—until she didn't.

Her condition was incurable, we were told, but with proper care she could live five to ten years. We did not share that with anybody. It wasn't time. We didn't want to burden anyone, particularly our girls, who were entering their senior year in high school. But "five to ten years" quickly turned into "two to four months," and we knew then that the girls had to know. That turned into "two weeks." The doctors said experimental treatments might have given her more time—but months, not years.

Theresa told us that it was time for her to go. She stopped treatments.

No book can tell you how to raise your two teenage girls after you've lost your wife in their senior year of high school. I could have used such a book.

We had had a traditional marriage. Theresa was the girls' primary caregiver, even though my travel schedule had decreased. I'd like to think I was a strong supporting actor, but Theresa had the main role at home. I was the primary breadwinner, though Theresa still worked part-time. She was the mom who could take the girls to activities and do the shopping. I was an 8 to 5:30 kind of guy. I could get to the girls' games, but I couldn't take them there.

And now I was called to pick up the pieces and carry on. I still had to be the dad and the breadwinner and run my new practice, and I was barely a year into that. And I had to make sure my girls got the devoted attention they deserved and needed. They needed to finish high school strong, to go to college, to thrive.

Anyone who has lost a loved one understands the stress. "How will I go on? How will I afford to live, to raise the kids alone?" I can help others plan so that they can deal with the financial impact. That's a matter of math. I cannot plan for how they will get through the tears. That's a matter of the heart.

I know now that the gift I can offer my clients is to take away the strain of financial worries so that they can focus on the mourning and the healing. I cannot heal their hearts, but I can certainly help them ease any financial burden so that they can attend to what matters most and make the most of their time. I can offer the gift of planning and security to tackle many of life's ups and downs, in a way that honors my clients' values and goals.

CALCULATING THE COSTS

Our family experience underscores the importance of thorough and comprehensive planning. Very early, I set goals for myself, and one of those was acquiring adequate life insurance. This included not only the proper type for my circumstance, but the correct amount.

One must be vigilant of the risk that dying too soon can pose to one's family. You should acquire insurance as early as you can, before any crisis or health issues arise. If you wait, you may not be able to get what you need. You will appreciate the coverage if you need it—and may regret that you didn't get more.

People drastically underestimate the amount of money they're going to need in retirement, and they drastically underestimate the amount of insurance needed if a spouse dies prematurely, whether a breadwinner or a homemaker. You might have $100,000 or $200,000 worth of coverage on your spouse and think that's enough, but that money will go quickly. Couples do not always recognize the extent of each other's contributions, both financially and non-financially.

A lot of analysis with regard to life insurance involves the human economic benefit. That means, for most people: "If I lose you and your earnings, how much money will I need to replace for how long?" But often, one spouse takes care of most of the day-to-day tasks, chores, and errands of running the household. That's a huge economic benefit. Until there's nobody there to do those things for you, it's hard to fully understand and appreciate the value. I know.

I also ask clients another basic question: "Would you still want to meet the goals that you have set out even if you weren't here?" That might seem like an odd question, but it gets to an important point: How much of the financial plan is "only if you live" and how much of it is "no matter what happens." Most people still want their spouse to be able to retire on time and live comfortably. They still want their children to be educated. They still want to be able to benefit causes that they care about.

It's not easy to prepare yourself emotionally for the loss of a loved one. It's unlikely you will be spending a lot of time in therapy getting ready to deal with that possibility. Though I can't help with the emotional part, I certainly can help with the financial preparation and calculations. Once those arrangements are made, you will be able to breathe easier knowing that you will be able to focus on your grief and healing in the event you endure such a loss. If your financial house is in order, you won't have to worry about money.

For some, grief is immediate and quick. Others may not feel it fully for months. It's hard to project the course of those emotions.

But you can project the course of the money, and that can be done in advance by setting up "what if" scenarios.

One of THE 6 BIG RISKS®, then, is dying too soon. It can be devastating to lose the one with whom you were anticipating a long life together, discussing your mutual values and goals, creating a financial roadmap. We all know people who have suffered such a loss. The emotional impact can be far reaching. The financial impacts can have significant consequences, as well.

The good news is that it is quite simple to plan the financial aspects. Grief must take its uncertain course, but in the meantime one thing is for sure: A well-designed and executed survivor plan can bring a significant amount of comfort to the family.

CHAPTER 2

LIVING TOO LONG

No one is really concerned about living too long, but a great many are concerned about outliving their money. As more and more people live longer, active, and healthy lives, they may need to plan for three decades of continuing consumption after concluding their working years.

In addition, most people have a list of interesting and exciting things that they intend to accomplish once they have the time and the freedom to do so. The reality is that the first decade of retirement can be pretty expensive.

A number of years ago, I saw a report in USA Today that listed what Americans fear most—such as fear of flying, of spiders, of divorce, and so on. The number-one fear, by far, was outliving their money. I can tell you that it certainly is a justified fear. Many people understand that they likely will live a lot longer than their money might last. They may have come to the realization that the lifestyle they imagined for themselves in retirement may not be achievable.

This is the crux of the distribution considerations of retirement planning. Not only do you need to accumulate enough money, but you also need to develop the necessary strategies for using those resources. How will you withdraw your money in a tax-efficient manner so that you can achieve all your goals, while protecting yourself from the potential for volatile market conditions during the decades of your retirement? How do you do that with some modicum of confidence that you will not run out of money?

There are some great strategies for making that work, but they are multi-disciplined: No single idea or product will provide you that security. That's why you need to be working with a professional who truly understands retirement income distribution and can help you to maximize your results.

It's important to see the grand context. What does the accumulation phase of life look like compared with the distribution phase? We typically spend the first 22 years of our lives growing up and getting an education; then three to eight years getting established in a career; and then, perhaps, getting married and having children. That pattern often has been established by the time people are in their 30s.

Most people like to retire in their early to mid-60s, so they have a working career of 35 years or so to build up the resources that probably must last them for two to three decades or longer of distribution. You have to accumulate not only enough to live on during those working years, but you also need to regularly save a portion of that money to fund an extended retirement.

It's ironic that living too long would arise as an issue in people's minds as they contemplate retirement. The primal fear, one would think, would be fear of dying. That change of perspective is a result of our changing demographics and highlights the need for adequate planning. The odds are that one spouse or the other will live many, many years in retirement, and both will need a continuing income.

It used to be that people retired for about 10 to 15 years and then dropped dead. When I started in this business in 1991, the combined life expectancy for men and women was about age 75; today, it is nearly 79. More and more people are living vibrant lives far longer than that. I have clients in their 90s.

That means more people will be spending as much time in retirement as they did in their working life. If you start your financial planning late, you have a problem to overcome. And by late, I mean age 40. If you're 55, you are really late. If you start at 40 and plan to retire at 65, your financial plan will only be working for you for 25 years until retirement—and then it very well may need to work an additional 25 years or more. Clearly, people are expecting the output of their financial plan to be much greater than the input—and therefore that input needs to really have some juice to it.

CHAPTER 3

BECOMING SICK OR INJURED

S tatistically, you are more likely to face a disability during your working years than a premature death. Unfortunately, planning for a disability event is at the bottom of the list of financial priorities for most people—if it is on that list at all.

There are three significant issues to consider if you are disabled during your working years. These three issues are what we call the "Financial Triple Whammy!"

The first is the fact that you will not be bringing in your normal income, yet your living expenses are likely to continue at a rate that is close to normal or higher. You also could face unplanned and uncovered out-of-pocket medical expenses and have to pay deductibles, co-pays, and the like.

The second issue is that there is a real possibility that you may have to dip into savings or your long-term nest egg in order to meet month-to-month living expenses. This is a good reason to have a robust emergency savings plan.

And the third issue is that without the ability to earn an income, your ability to participate in retirement savings or tax qualified plans could be diminished or eliminated, depending on the severity and length of your disability.

A HARD TRUTH

Of course, people with disabilities can live long and productive lives and contribute so very much to society. We all can cite examples of that. Society has taken great strides in accommodating them and making the most of their true talents.

But the fact remains that a disability can be a drain on your resources, and you have to plan for that potential. If you have a particular skill set, the disability could prevent you from making a living that way any longer. For some occupations, physical strength and agility are crucial; other occupations depend on mental or sensory capacity. If you need to redefine your career due to a disability, you may feel a significant impact on your income.

I believe that most people, if they were to ask themselves whether they would rather die or suffer a disability, would conclude that it depended upon the disability. Clearly, some disabilities infringe more than others on quality of life, and a long-term disability can be far more devastating financially than a death.

The good news is there are cost-effective ways to plan around the risk of a disability. Still, this tends to be an unspoken topic. When a family faces a death, the impact is more pronounced. It feels more devastating, but there is often a sense of closure—a memorial service, a funeral. But who goes to a memorial service for a disability?

People can live for decades after sustaining a disability and have no ability to take care of themselves. This is a hard truth to face. Medical science has blessed us with longer lives, but we have to pay for the continued care.

LONG-TERM CARE NEEDS

Once you have retired, assuming you have planned well to fund a vibrant lifestyle, the risk you face is one of a long-term care event. With the cost of quality care in the $70,000 per year range and rising, and the average stay in a care facility approaching three years, ask yourself what the financial impact of a $200,000 depletion of assets would do to the quality of life of those whom you leave behind?

This is a subject with a lot of emotion attached to it ranging from, "My family will take care of me," to, "I really don't care; I'll fund it when the time comes."

I offer the following two professional observations:

1. If you can't afford the premium, then you certainly can't afford the event.
   - If you can't afford a few hundred dollars a month, how are you going to afford thousands of dollars a month?
2. Even if you have the money to self-insure, why would you?
   - It is almost always more cost effective to transfer the risk than to reserve it for yourself.

The problem with self-insuring is the opportunity cost. If you are reserving $200,000, that means it cannot be used for other things. You can't spend it to do or buy things that might support your retirement goals. You cannot invest it and put it at risk in the market— meaning you would be losing the potential to gain $16,000 a year if the market returned 8 percent. Instead, you have to cordon off that sum and keep it safe. Even if you could get a 2 percent return on such an investment and make $4,000, your opportunity cost still would be $12,000.

In other words, you can say you will self-insure so that you don't have to pay a premium—but you will be paying that premium nonetheless. The premium that you're paying is $1,000 a month ($12,000 opportunity cost divided by 12 months in a year). And you typically can get you a far better policy for much less than $1,000 a month.

CHAPTER 4

IMPROPER TAX PLANNING

Before you receive your pay, you have deductions for federal taxes, Social Security, Medicare, state and local taxes, workers' compensation, and more, depending on your particular situation. And then we pay sales taxes, property taxes, and those taxes and fees on your cell phone bill, on your cable bill, on your water bill, on your gas bill, on your electric bill. A myriad of levies are embedded in the cost of gasoline. The list of taxes goes on and on.

Improper tax planning is costly. Citizens must pay their legally required taxes, of course, but there is no need to send the government any more money than required. The IRS code is full of opportunities for those who are looking.

When it comes to taxation, it is important not only to understand where you stand today but also what your situation will be in 3, 5, 10, and 20 years from now. We will need to make some reasonable assumptions and projections to see what the impact of taxation might be on you.

TAX-INFESTED RETIREMENT ACCOUNTS

The IRA was developed on the theory that you should defer taxes now because when you're in retirement you'll be in a lower tax bracket. Do you really think that will be the case? Why would you want to be making less money when you retire? The idea of proactive financial planning is to ensure your wealth in retirement—and more wealth means more tax.

When it comes to retirement plans, remember that the government giveth and the government taketh away. When you open your IRA or 401(k) statement, you may be proud of the number—but are you aware that not all that money is yours? The government has a lien on it, and it's called taxation. The portion of that account that's not yours depends on your tax bracket.

Let's just say you start investing in an IRA account at the age of 22 and do that for 45 years until retiring at age 67. At $5,500 a year, in 45 years you will have put away just under $250,000. For the sake of argument, let's say it has grown to more than $4 million.

Depending on your circumstances, you might choose between a traditional IRA and a Roth IRA. The difference is how that money is going to be treated.

In a traditional, tax-deferred account, you would subtract that $5,500 from your annual income to reduce the amount subject to taxation. You pay no tax until you withdraw the money in retirement. In a Roth account, you get no tax break up front for that $5,500 deposit, but you are not taxed upon withdrawal.

....

Let's look at it how our example works in each account, with $250,000 in contributions, the same rate of return, and an end value of $4 million.

In a traditional IRA, the annual income is reduced by $5,500 every year. If you're in the 25 percent tax bracket, you will have saved $1,375 every year for 45 years. You have saved almost $62,000 in income tax. However, your $4 million account has a tax lien on it. Every dollar you take out of that account is going to be taxed. Let's assume for now that it's at the same rate as when you put it away. So, 25 percent of $4 million is a million dollars.

So basically what you did was you traded $62,000 of tax savings during your working years, so that you could pay $1 million in tax in your retirement years.

And consider this: If you had a $4 million account, do you think you will only be paying 25 percent tax? I would suggest to you that your tax rate might be 33 percent or higher. You could potentially be in the highest tax bracket in this nation, which is currently 39.6, plus 3.8 percent Medicare surtax, or in excess of 43 percent.

That's how the government taketh away.

Now let's compare that to the Roth account. You did not take the $1,375 tax savings every year. You paid the tax on that $5,500 and gave up $62,000 worth of tax savings—that is, $1,375 a year for a 45-year working career. Here's the difference: That $4 million Roth IRA is free from all tax. Every dollar you take out of that account is yours.

In essence, there is a tax lien on your traditional IRA and 401(k) assets—and that lien has an adjustable rate. You don't know what the tax rate will be upon withdrawal, but you might presume at least 43 percent. I call those "tax-infested" accounts. If you have a tax-infested retirement account, you are going to need a strategy to maximize the amount of money you get out and minimize the amount of taxation.

For many years, the government has been quite kind to savers and investors, with a liberal limit to what you can put away tax-deferred or even tax-free. But as the government faces pressure from deficits and interest on its debts, it will be looking for revenue sources to fund its liabilities. You can assume that these accounts will be under review.

That's why you need a tax strategy that works for you. You want to be invested for your future, not infested.

A TALE ABOUT TAXES

One of my favorite examples about our tax system was sent to me some years ago by a colleague.

Suppose that every day, ten men go out for lunch and the bill for all ten comes to $100. If they paid their bill the way we pay for our taxes, it would go something like this:

- The first four men (the poorest) would pay nothing.

- The fifth would pay $1.
- The sixth would pay $3.
- The seventh would pay $7.
- The eighth would pay $12.
- The ninth would pay $18.
- The tenth man (the richest) would pay $59.

So, that's what they decided to do.

The ten men ate lunch in the restaurant every day and seemed quite happy with the arrangement, until one day, the owner threw them a curve ball.

"Since you are such good customers," he said, "I'm going to reduce the cost of your daily lunch by $20." So lunch for the ten men would now cost just $80.

The group still wanted to pay their bill the way we pay our taxes. So, the first four men were unaffected. They would still eat for free. But what about the other six men? How could they divide the $20 windfall so that everyone would get his fair share?

They realized that $20 divided by six is $3.33. But if they subtracted that from everybody's share, then the fifth and sixth man would each end up being paid to eat his lunch.

So the restaurant owner suggested that it would be fair to reduce each man's bill by a higher percentage the poorer he was, to follow the principle of the tax system they had been using, and he proceeded to work out the amounts he suggested that each man should now pay. And so:

- The fifth man, like the first four, now paid nothing (100% off).
- The sixth now paid $2 instead of $3 (33% off).
- The seventh now paid $5 instead of $7 (28% off).
- The eighth now paid $9 instead of $12 (25% off).
- The ninth now paid $14 instead of $18 (22% off).
- The tenth now paid $49 instead of $59 (18% off).

Each of the six was better off than before. And the first four continued to eat lunch for free. But, once outside the bar, the men began to compare the amount they got off.

The sixth man said, "I only got $1 out of the $20, while the tenth man got $10!"

"Yeah, that's right," exclaimed the fifth man. "I only got $1 off, too. It's unfair that he got ten times more benefit than me."

"That's true," shouted the seventh man. "Why should he get $10 off, when I got only $2? The wealthy get all the breaks!"

"Wait a minute," yelled the first four men in unison, "we didn't get anything at all. The new tax system exploits the poor!"

The nine men surrounded the tenth and told him that they were angry that he got so much off while they each got very little.

The next day, the tenth man didn't show up for lunch, so the nine sat down and had their lunches without him. But when it came time to pay the bill, they discovered something important. They didn't have enough money among them for even half the bill!

And that is how our tax system works. The people who already pay the highest taxes will naturally get the largest benefit from a tax reduction. Tax them too much, attack them for being wealthy, and they just may not show up anymore. In fact, they might start eating their lunch overseas.

For those who understand, no explanation is needed. For those who do not understand, no explanation is possible.

CHAPTER 5

LEGAL ENTANGLEMENTS

L ife, it has been said, is not measured by the number of breaths we take, but by the moments that take our breath away. I have experienced a rollercoaster of such moments, some momentous and some intimate, some pleasant and some painful—including the fall of the Berlin Wall, the birth of my twin daughters and their amazing success, the loss of Theresa, meeting Beth and falling in love a second time, and expanding my family with my sons Braxton and Bennett.

Through it all, I kept a legal plan in place in case something terrible were to happen to me unexpectedly. Until I did my own planning, the government had a plan for me. It's the same plan it has for you, if you haven't gotten around to making arrangements of your own. I can assure you that the default government plan is not as good as the one you could develop for yourself. You need to carefully consider how your affairs will be handled both while you are living and after you have passed.

Don't think legal planning is just for when you die. It's also for when you are living. We make that distinction by referring to "above-the-grass" planning and "below-the-grass" planning. In this chapter, we'll take a look at the former. I'll discuss estate planning in Part Three, Chapter 5.

ABOVE THE GRASS PLANNING™

A part of our Comprehensive Financial Solutions™, the Recurring Review Cycle™ program includes a review of your foundational legal documents, which we can help you to structure in coordination with an attorney, if necessary. Those documents include:

◆ Durable Power of Attorney for Legal and Financial matters
◆ Durable Power of Attorney for Medical and Health matters, including HIPAA compliance
◆ Living Will (also known as a Health Care Directive)
◆ Revocable Living Trusts

We live in a complex world, and a good idea can have ramifications that were never intended. For example, HIPPA (the Health Insurance Portability and Accountability Act) is designed to protect patient information, but it also can impact a spouse's or a child's ability to access information or to direct care.

That's one good reason to do some above-the-grass planning. What happens if you are still alive but unable to act on your own behalf? You may be in a coma or otherwise unable to communicate, or you may not have the mental capacity to do so. Who is going to handle your affairs? You cannot just assume that it will be your closest loved ones, or your spouse, or your child. To take away any ambiguity, we recommend that you designate powers of attorney for specific items, such as legal, financial, and health-care issues.

You may choose to have a single power of attorney that does all of them. Or you may have a family member who is a medical professional or is particularly caring, and you want that person to be responsible for all of your health-care decisions. Another member of your family may be particularly savvy on financial or legal affairs. Nothing says that you can't have three separate powers of attorney with specific designations of responsibility. You can grant the authority either immediately or have it take effect once you are deemed incapacitated by a medical professional. I prefer the latter.

BUSINESS STRUCTURE

As part of your above-the-grass planning, you also need to protect against legal entanglements. If you're self-employed or you own a business, how should that be legally structured? Should it be a limited liability company? Should it be a partnership? Should it be a corporation? If it's a corporation should it be a C-corp or an S-corp? Do you have a Buy-Sell agreement? Does it cover disability, as well as death? These (and many more) questions need to be answered by two professionals: a business entity attorney, and a CPA, in coordination with your financial planner.

A lot of people own property, and some of that property may be a primary residence and some may be a vacation home, or rental property. What sort of liability are you taking with doing that? Are those the sorts of things that should be in a limited liability company? How much of your personal wealth and your personal assets do you want to expose to someone who trips and falls on your rental property? If the business is not properly structured, you could lose everything.

Unless you carefully consider these matters and take action to set yourself up properly, you could be sued for all you're worth. You need to shield yourself. You deserve a bulletproof financial plan.

CHAPTER 6

THE BIGGEST RISK OF ALL ...

In 1980, I was living in Ellensburg, Washington, a town east of the Cascades. My dad, an accomplished musician and music teacher, was finishing his master's degree in conducting.

Because I was brought up to make my own way, I had a job as a dishwasher at the Holiday Inn, to which I rode my bike several miles. I often came home late at night, which was safe in a small town in those days. I enjoyed skiing, and that's how I paid for it.

On Saturday, May 17, 1980, I'd had a rather uneventful shift at work, and I got off about midnight. The next day, my dad had an important recital, and we planned a reception in the backyard of our rented home. It was a big day for him. My parents had planned the party for weeks, and Sunday morning was crunch time.

It was pitch black outside when I rolled into bed, but when I awoke, it still seemed dark. I looked at my alarm—it said 9 o'clock. Had I slept through the big day? Why would my parents just let me sleep until evening?

I went downstairs and found my mom busily preparing for the party. "It's so dark out," she said. "I think it's going to storm. How are we ever going to fit all those people inside this tiny house?"

I stepped outside to see whether it was raining—and saw that it was raining ash. It covered the street, the grass, everything. Mount Saint Helens had erupted.

When I think of that day, and how I found myself in darkness and confusion, I am reminded of the financial risks that so many people face every day. They might be small risks that build up to a major problem, with warning signs along the way, or they might be sudden and cataclysmic.

One never knows, and one must be prepared. If you fail to do effective financial planning, you just might awaken to darkness one day.

So what is the biggest risk of all? ...

It's an uncoordinated financial plan!

THE FIVE KEY FINANCIAL DISCIPLINES

To effectively manage your finances, you need to keep in mind and coordinate the five key disciplines. We have been discussing these throughout this book:

1. Risk Management

2. Wealth Management
3. Financial Planning
4. Tax Planning
5. Legal Planning

Let's say you interviewed a hundred people on the street. How many could name all five disciplines? Of those, how many would have sought out experts in each area? And of those, how many would have actually listened to those experts and followed their advice?

As you might expect, the answer is very few indeed. Most people are in the dark when it comes to naming these five principles, and they also well might be at financial risk. Effective financial planning requires coordination of various professionals so that each isn't doing his or her work in a silo. Somebody has to be responsible for weaving the thread of continuity through all of the disciplines. This will help ensure that clients' most important goals are in complete alignment with their most deeply held values.

A TEAM APPROACH

When is the last time your insurance agent, wealth manager, financial planner, attorney, and CPA sat in the same room to discuss your individual financial plan? Do they even know who the other professionals on your team are?

Despite their expertise, they need to communicate. A professional in one field can produce excellent, beautifully crafted, technically correct work that is in conflict with another professional's excellent, beautifully crafted, and technically correct work.

The result is a hodgepodge of ideas that do not support your most important goals and is not in alignment with your most deeply held values.

Most professionals are classically trained in their particular discipline. Unfortunately, that means they do things their own way. Most don't ask the right questions as it pertains to an overall financial plan.

There has been more than one occasion in my professional career where I have seen a plan drafted by a CPA that is in conflict with a plan that an attorney drafted. The two of them never spoke.

A financial planner really can't rely on the client to be that bridge. It would be like a primary care physician insisting that a patient relay detailed diagnostic information to a specialist for the development of a proper course of treatment. That would be absurd. The experts must communicate directly with each other. And someone must coordinate the experts to make sure they are working together efficiently.

WHO'S THE HEAD COACH?

If you were the owner of a professional sports franchise, you could hire a head coach to coordinate all of the specialty team coaches and players on the field. You could simply tell them what you want to achieve—a better record than last year, going to the divisional playoffs, or winning the big show. Their job is to worry about the day-to-day and to make it happen.

As head coach for my clients, my job is to look at that roster of professionals on the team. The clients tell me what they want to achieve, and then they go enjoy their life. They get to sit in the box seat and watch the results that I get for them.

Be sure your advisor or ensemble team has the expertise and resources to be the head coach of your financial plan. A financial planner requires the leadership abilities to coordinate all of those players, many of whom have egos. He or she must know enough about each of those particular disciplines to recognize when it is time to call in a specialist.

PART THREE

ANATOMY OF A FINANCIAL PLAN

It's time now to take a tour through the structure of a comprehensive financial plan. This will involve the actual coordination of those five disciplines, any one of which could be the subject of an entire book: Risk Management, Wealth Management, Financial Planning, Tax Planning, and Estate Planning.

These high-level concepts are easy to understand, though they may seem complex. My goal is to make financial planning clear and understandable. What is difficult for many is putting all the pieces together to execute the concepts and maintaining a sense of accountability.

I cannot emphasize enough that financial planning is *not* wealth management. Wealth management is certainly an important part of an overall, comprehensive financial plan. But it's just one part. At some point in your life, you are likely to need all five of these disciplines. You will need them to be working well individually, but you will also need them to be working well in concert. As you cobble together a financial plan, it can seem just too complicated to handle. But when you break it down into its components, it becomes easier.

You need, in effect, someone to conduct the orchestra.

CHAPTER 1

MANAGING THE RISKS

It's not much fun to talk about all those risks that one faces in life and finances—but it is critical to understand them, because they can scuttle the best-laid plan.

When I talk about risk management, I include anything that could potentially derail your financial plan. When most people think of risk management, they're thinking purely about insurances. But remember that the things that insurance protects against are not the only risks to your financial welfare.

As we have discussed in previous chapters, for example, you face the risk of unnecessarily paying more taxes than the government requires of you, and you face a variety of legal risks that must be examined in your "above the grass" and "below the grass" planning. Your income itself also could be at risk. We assess the reliability of your income, looking at all the sources, how stable they are, and what protective measures are in place.

Let's take a look at insurances first. Most people have experience with property and casualty insurance. They have auto and homeowner policies that protect against damage or loss and against liability up to a specified amount, and they may carry an umbrella policy for additional or broader coverage.

Those policies should be regularly reviewed in a financial plan—as well as the policies that you purchase to protect against loss of life and disability.

LIFE INSURANCE

While you're accumulating an estate, you need to protect against the fact that you don't yet have an estate. In other words, you still want to provide dollars for your survivors even if you do not have time to accumulate enough money to provide for them. You want to meet their basic needs as well as assist them in achieving goals.

Life insurance also can be used for its potential to preserve an estate. This is particularly important if you have accumulated an estate that is illiquid. The government can be impatient when it comes to wanting to collect its money. It doesn't matter if all of your money is tied up in a beautiful home or a family ranch or business. It has an assessed value for tax purposes, and the government wants its cut.

Life insurance companies are astute at business—and their business is to mitigate risk. I like to refer to them as risk merchants. They know how to make a profit—and that, of course, is what you want. Would you trust an insurance company that wasn't profitable?

When the chips are down, and you need that insurance company, you will want it to be a sound business that is financially stable.

You will often hear people demonizing insurance companies, but let me assure you that they are well regulated. They are required by law to have levels of reserve that are far higher than a bank or the federal government must have.

In considering life insurance, ask yourself these questions as you begin to assess the type and amount you will need:

- Do I have outstanding liabilities that would burden those I left behind?
- What would the economic impact be to my family if I weren't here?
- Would all of the goals that I have set be accomplished? Is that important to me?
- How long is the period of risk that the life insurance should cover?
- Who will be the beneficiaries of the policy?

DISABILITY

You will also want to seriously consider your need for disability insurance, as I discussed in Part 2, Chapter 3, "THE 6 BIG RISKS®." The need for disability insurance can come at various times in your life—both in your working years and in your retirement years.

Statistically, you are more likely to become disabled during your working life than you are to die prematurely. Yet most people, if they were to carry one of those two coverages, will carry life insurance and not disability.

Classic disability coverage replaces income or a portion of income. Have you considered how you will replace your lack of ability to contribute to a 401(k) or an IRA? If you have business obligations, how will you continue? How will you keep the lights on? There are strategies to address each of these questions.

In retirement, disability insurance often takes the form of long-term care coverage. From a financial planner's perspective, here is the major advantage of long-term care insurance: If I know that you have that benefit available to you, that means I don't have to reserve for that in your retirement distribution plan. And as a result, it will allow you the freedom and flexibility to spend more money in retirement.

As I pointed out earlier: If you cannot afford the premium, you cannot afford the event. Even if you can afford to self-insure and have enough money to set aside in case you need long-term care, you are losing out on other things that you could do with that money.

OTHER MAJOR RISKS

Besides the risks that you can cover through insurance or through diligent tax and legal planning, you should be aware of some other risks to your wealth.

Identity-theft protection: Some financial planners never talk about this with regard to risk management. At our firm, we take very seriously the fact that you could face cyber-security threats. We highly recommend, for example, that clients use two credit cards—one for shopping, whether at stores or online, and another that is used exclusively for recurring charges and that never sees the light of day.

To protect yourself against identity theft, you can hire a company to monitor your status in cyber-space. Many protection companies advertise on the Internet, and I personally have subscribed for many years to a well-known one. Or you could do it yourself—although most people, I believe, would do well to focus on other things in life. If you do take on that responsibility, you will need to review your credit on a regular basis, over a variety of channels, including credit card companies and bank accounts, and you will need to request and examine your credit report annually.

Electronic data backup: Another risk that we face in our digital world is the potential for loss of our electronic records. Data backup is essential. So many aspects of our lives are digital today. It used to be that we wanted to protect our photo albums. For most people today, the "photo album" has become digital. Are you using a backup?

As with identity theft issues, you can either delegate the job or you can take it upon yourself. You can hire somebody to provide the service of constantly backing up all of your data, all of the time. There are many firms that will do that for you. Or, if you have the time and discipline, you can manually make sure that your records are backed up, either locally or in the cloud.

Password list: I like my clients to have what I call a consolidated master password list. If something happened to you, would your spouse know how to get into all of your accounts? What is the website? What is your username? What is the password? What is the site key? What are the answers to the challenge questions? Do you have them written down or tracked digitally via LastPass, 1Password, etc.?

Whatever your method, you should communicate that information to your loved ones and to your planning team. I typically recommend to clients that they, at a minimum, have a written list locked away someplace. I like to put that in a password-protected Excel file that I also store in the cloud, so that my wife has access to that information should we need it. It has a sheet for each of us. There are also services that can memorize your passwords; the information is kept readily available, and the service will log you in to sites that you use regularly.

As you can see, risk management goes far beyond the typical considerations with which most insurance salespeople deal. A professional in comprehensive financial planning can step you through the variety of risks that often escape people's attention.

CHAPTER 2

INVESTING FOR YOUR FUTURE

If there's any element of financial planning that people get excited about, it's wealth management. But wealth management, as we have seen, is divided into the accumulation and distribution phases. Some advisors are so focused on the accumulation phase that they really don't understand all of the issues associated with the distribution phase.

When you are investing for your future, you must consider the six key principles that we discussed in Chapter 3 of Part 1:

1. How early you start investing
2. How often you invest
3. How much you invest
4. Whether you stay invested
5. How much you keep (avoiding tax erosion)
6. Your rate of return

Think of your assets as being in two primary buckets. In one would be your non-tax-qualified investments, and in the other one would be your tax-qualified investments. People tend to get confused about the difference between the registration of an account and what the account is using as an investment vehicle. An IRA, for example, is a registration. It is not an investment vehicle. People will say, "I have a mutual fund, and I have an IRA." What they likely have are two mutual funds, one of which is held in an IRA.

There are many ways to register an account. What sort of registrations might you have? You could have an account that's registered in just your name, or in the name of both your spouse and you jointly with rights of survivorship, or JTWROS. An account could be registered to John Doe as custodian for little Jane Doe, through the Uniform Transfers to Minors Act, or UTMA. An IRA can be registered to an individual's benefit, as can a 401(k) or 403(b) or a 457 plan. Those are types of account registrations.

INVESTMENT OPTIONS

Once you get beyond that, you then consider your investment options and the vehicles that you could use—such as mutual funds, individual stocks, exchange-traded funds, managed futures, commodities, precious metals, and investments that are geographically focused like, global, international, emerging-market, or U.S. domestic. Some investments are equity oriented while some are fixed income oriented, or a combination of both.

The universe of investment options is vast. It is important to be working with a professional who has access to all of them and who can tailor the recommendations to what is in your best interest.

The purpose of this book is not to recommend whether you should be invested in equities or in bonds or in domestic or foreign stocks. It would be unwise, in fact, to make such a general pronouncement, since each individual has a unique situation.

Just as there are many ways to accumulate for the future, there are many ways to distribute for your retirement. Again, in making such decisions, we must keep in mind the registration of the account, versus the investment vehicle that underlies it.

For example, there are a number of ways to effectively accumulate money for a college education. In the past, the only options were savings bonds or through the Uniform Gifts to Minors Act / Uniform Transfer to Minors Act (UGMA/UTMA). Then, the government instituted educational savings accounts. Today, the 529 account has pretty much displaced all other means of saving for college.

(By the way, all those numbers and letters, as in 401(k), and 403(b), and 457, and 529, are simply paragraphs in the Internal Revenue Code. Those are the paragraphs that reference the rules associated with particular registrations.)

I do not believe, however, that you should withdraw from your retirement plan to pay for college expenses, even when you can do so without penalty for early withdrawal. I don't agree with provisions allowing such withdrawals for educational purposes or for a first house purchase. Those accumulation programs are meant for your retirement. It's your biggest investment in life, and you must not let anything sap the power of the compounding.

I also doubt the wisdom of a 401(k) loan to yourself. Such loans are rarely repaid. Despite their best intentions, people end up paying the penalty and taxes. The loan hurts them more than it ever helped them. I have seen far too many people who put the full funding of their child's education in front of their own retirement. I'm not sure that's the wisest thing to do. If you have the financial means to pay for all of it, fine. But think hard before sacrificing your ability to retire.

A POSTPENSION RETIREMENT

Once, people would dedicate 30 or 40 years of their life to a particular company and then get a pension for life that represented much of the pay they had received while working. Certainly in conjunction with Social Security benefits, they would have a very comfortable retirement.

The days of the defined benefit plan are nearly gone. That hasn't changed because companies are mean. Rather, we should all be rejoicing for the reason: We are living longer. And actuarially, companies cannot put enough money away from a worker's salary to pay benefits for decades after that person stops working.

Social Security and many pension plans were based upon the fact that most people would probably only live a few years after retiring at age 65. As that statistic has changed, more of the onus for retirement security falls on the individual as companies have switched to defined contribution plans.

In a 401(k), as an example, every worker in 2015 has the ability to put away $18,000 per year. In addition, the employer can put additional money into the employer's side of the 401(k), which then can be matched up to a particular percentage or a threshold. And that threshold is pretty high. The total amount of money that you can put in an employer plan in 2015 is $53,000. Of that, you would contribute $18,000, and you and your employer would put in the balance through matching contributions, etc. If you are 50 or older, you have catch-up provisions in an employer plan allowing you to put away an additional $6,000 per year or $24,000, versus $18,000. In many plans, you can choose whether your plan will be a traditional one or a Roth.

In addition, everybody, regardless of income (even Bill Gates), is eligible to contribute to an IRA. Those limits are $5,500 per year, and if you're 50 or over, you can put in an additional $1,000. Whether that contribution is deductible or not is based on a variety of factors, such as income and retirement plan participation. Eligibility for a Roth IRA is largely income dependent, but there are strategies that allow individuals over the income limits to contribute to a Roth. This is due to Congress permanently repealing the once $100,000 annual limit for Roth conversions.

If your employer plan allows you to have a Roth 401(k), strongly consider it, as income limits do not restrict your participation in the same way they do for a personal Roth IRA. If your plan doesn't permit Roth 401(k) contributions, ask your payroll department to have the plan document amended to add it—it is a very straightforward procedure for any company.

Which should you choose—a traditional account or a Roth? As with many questions in financial planning, the answer is: "It depends." It depends on your individual circumstances and goals. But understand that you are eligible for such plans. There's no excuse for anyone not to be putting enough money away. Even if you have maxed out your 401(k) and your individual IRA contributions, there are other ways to accumulate even more money on a tax-deferred basis—although those tend to be for very high income earners. That's for another book and another time.

A TAX STRATEGY FOR WITHDRAWAL

This is my advice for most of my readers and clients: In your accumulation years, do all you can to get as much money as possible into your employer plan, and then we'll talk about what's next. You will have plenty of opportunities ahead, but it's important to understand that assets come in three varieties when it comes to tax treatment. Whether an asset is always-taxed, tax-deferred, or tax advantaged should play a major role in investment decisions.

The Roth accounts fall into the tax advantaged category. You pay income tax on the money before you put it into the plan, but all of the distribution is free from taxation. The traditional IRA and 401(k) style accounts are tax-deferred, meaning the amount you contribute is shielded from immediate taxation, but during your retirement you will pay tax on all the withdrawals. In some plans, you have a choice on whether the part you are contributing will be tax-deferred or tax-free. On the employer contribution side of a 401(k), however, you don't have a choice. The rules require that portion to be tax-deferred.

A great many accounts fall into the always-taxed category. Those include regular savings, brokerage, and managed accounts. When you post earnings and have distributions, even if you reinvest them, the government will presume that you have taken "constructive receipt" of the money, and it will want its tax on the amount of that gain. The government does not care what you did with the money. It sees a taxable income and wants its portion.

As you make your investment decisions for your future, therefore, you need to pay close attention to developing a strategy for how the money will eventually be distributed. And that's why you need a planner with extensive experience in dealing not just with accumulation but with distribution for retirement.

CHAPTER 3

RETIREMENT INCOME PLANNING

I ncome planning is where we start to talk about cash flow—the money coming in and the money going out. Just as you plan during your working years for how you will obtain the money to fund your lifestyle, so too you need to find the best way to tap into your savings efficiently to fund your retirement lifestyle.

As you're developing your accumulation strategy, you need to keep the exit strategy in mind. What will the sources of your retirement income be, and what will be the tax impact of withdrawing money from your various accounts?

A major consideration is when you should turn on your Social Security benefit. Should you take it early, at age 62, or wait until 66 or 70? If you are married, can you take advantage of a strategy to coordinate the timing for maximum benefit?

Such planning can get complicated, but a good financial planner can help you determine all of the income that will be available from a variety of sources. Besides Social Security, some clients have pensions, and some have traditional or Roth IRAs and 401(k)s. Some will be able to liquidate real estate, and some might have inheritances and trust income and other sources. All those income streams need to be mapped and put through a tax filter to find out the best way to create that retirement "paycheck."

One thing that irritates many of our clients is the "RMD" (required minimum distribution) from their tax-deferred retirement plans. Many people who have saved and invested have done so with such discipline that they have accumulated far more money than they will ever need. They would prefer that the money stay in the account and grow, but they struck a deal back when they started to contribute to the plan. The government allowed them to defer taxes at the time, but now, in retirement, it demands that they withdraw an increasingly large amount each year and pay taxes on it. The account is likely to be liquidated by the time they are in their 90s. The government wants all the tax back that it allowed them to defer, and more.

That raises the question about whether you should convert your traditional retirement plan into a Roth IRA by immediately paying the taxes due. First, nobody should use the retirement account itself to fund the conversion. In other words, don't take money out of an IRA prematurely in order to pay the tax to convert to a Roth as withdrawals prior to age 59 1/2 may result in a 10% IRA penalty tax. You should only be considering a conversion if there are other sources of income.

It really can make a whole lot of sense, however, to pay the tax now so that you don't have to pay the tax later. How can you know whether it would work for you? The only way is to do income modeling based on the distribution and how it would impact other aspects of your planning.

Retirement income planning is its own discipline, with a lot of moving parts. You need to make sure that someone on your team understands all the implications of any decision you might wish to make.

CHAPTER 4

DEALING WITH UNCLE SAM

Our tax code is far from simple, but it does include breaks for those who employ the strategies to take advantage of them. Many people do not take full advantage of the tax code as it is written. Not only do they unnecessarily pay more in taxes than they are required, but an even greater concern is that they could be making decisions today that lead to greater taxation in the future.

There are many wonderful tax preparers. There are fewer tax planners. When considering your source of advice, ask yourself this question: "Am I working with a tax historian or with a tax visionary?" Most people in the tax profession are what I call tax historians. They are reporting to the government what has happened. They are not looking at what could be. You need someone who has a vision for how taxation will fit into the overall financial planning picture. In my experience, you need more than someone who is simply writing what amounts to a report card that they submit, on your behalf, to the IRS.

I like to work instead with visionaries. I like to work with tax planners—the type who, for example, understand the implications that deferring taxes today could have on your tax obligation tomorrow. A visionary planner can grasp right away the possibility that a Roth conversion might bring future savings that could more efficiently be passed on to heirs.

STRETCH PROVISIONS

When somebody other than a spouse inherits an IRA, that individual has a number of choices to make. He or she could take the money all at once, in a lump sum, or in a series of payments on a schedule.

Under what is known as a "stretch" provision, the recipient can take required minimum distributions from the inherited IRA, with the amount of those RMDs determined by life expectancy. So if a 40-year-old who inherits an IRA from a parent will be taking out small amounts on a regular basis, they will be required to begin those distributions a year after the date of the death.

However, the remaining balance of the inherited IRA will continue to grow tax-deferred. If it's a traditional IRA, they'll pay tax as the money comes out. But if it's a Roth IRA, not only will they only have to take out a small amount of money, but that money will also be tax-free. The remainder will continue to grow within the account and will not be subject to taxes upon withdrawal.

It's a phenomenal gift. It stretches the power of compounding across another generation, and the numbers can be mind-boggling.

PLANNING AT A PREMIUM

And something else is mind-boggling. Now and then, attempts are made to "simplify" the tax code, but as I was writing this book, three new tax laws came into effect that influenced taxes in seven ways based on three income levels and four different computations. That's our simplified tax code.

As the tax climate changes, the need for effective planning will be at a premium. Taxes certainly aren't going away, and I don't think they're going down. Inflation alone will lead to the phenomenon of "bracket creep" as people earn more money and enter the higher tax categories.

As you earn more money, many of the things that you thought were givens—such as your standard or itemized deductions, or how your Social Security and Medicare is taxed, or how much you can deduct for mortgage interest—start to get squeezed. You start to lose the ability to lower your effective income to get into a lower tax bracket.

And that's why I say that there's a premium on tax planning. You're going to need someone who understands not only the current impact of these rules and law changes but who also can anticipate any repercussions in five years or 30 years. How will these changes affect the transfer, ultimately, of your estate?

It's a serious matter. The manner in which your tax planning is handled could spell the difference between having a nice sum to leave to your heirs and running out of money before you run out of life.

CHAPTER 5

ESTATE OF AFFAIRS

Death is never easy, and yet it is inevitable. Theresa's death was heartbreaking, yet it was a time of connection. As she faced death, we held hands and talked about life. We talked about all that we had planned over the years, our dreams and aspirations, the future of our family.

It can be overwhelming to lose a loved one, and part of the stress comes from worrying about financial and legal affairs. A good financial plan reduces those fears so that you can focus on family.

Theresa and I addressed our legal, tax, and financial issues, and thoroughly discussed family matters and values. Both of us knew that I alone would be seeing things through, and so I listened to her intently. I didn't feel that I was wandering aimlessly after she passed. Even with a broken heart, I felt confident about what I was supposed to be doing. I had clarity about what was important to us as a couple. I felt a sense of calm.

I was becoming a single dad at a critical juncture in our daughters' lives and wanted to do this right. I had prided myself in being a good planner, and this most certainly would put that to the test. Much of my energy was devoted to carrying on with life and being the father I needed to be. I was able to do so knowing that matters of estate planning had already been given due consideration.

Estate planning involves a variety of considerations. Sometimes I hear people saying that they don't have enough money to be concerned about having an estate plan. What they don't realize is that they already have one, if they haven't taken action. It's the government's plan, and it is unlikely to be in their best interest. It tends to be expedient, and it tends to fall in the government's favor when there's any sort of ambiguity.

HOW ASSETS TRANSFER AFTER DEATH

Some people make presumptions such as "my spouse or my family will get everything." But that depends on a lot of things, including the laws and the probate process in your state. California, for example, has a particularly laborious probate process, while the state of Washington has a simplified process.

The government has also published reams of options that are available to anyone who would like to take advantage of them. Many of them are quite advantageous. They can significantly help out the next and future generations. Not only can you reduce tax exposure, but your affairs will also be directed according to your wishes, not by someone else's interpretation of your wishes. You can set forth exactly how and when things should happen.

Traditionally, people have a will. Most people have a very simple one, what's referred to as an "I love you" will, which basically says, "Everything that I have now goes to you." However, you cannot simply say you want everything to go to your spouse and expect that that will necessarily happen.

Assets transfer three ways: 1) by beneficiary designation; 2) by title; and 3) by will. Let's say you had a retirement plan from an employer that you started in your 20s but you left that employer in your 40s without transferring the retirement plan. You divorce and remarry, but your former spouse's name remains as beneficiary on that plan. You never changed the designation. Guess what? Your will does not trump the beneficiary designation form of a tax qualified plan or of a life insurance policy.

That has been fought without success all the way to the Supreme Court. Some attorneys believe that they can write language into a legal document that will usurp that, but they have not prevailed. A beneficiary form is king.

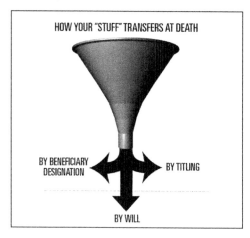

HOW YOUR "STUFF" TRANSFERS AT DEATH

BY BENEFICIARY DESIGNATION

BY TITLING

BY WILL

The next means of transfer is by title. Whose name is on the deed of the house? Let's say you own a lake house with your brother. The ownership is joint with rights of survivorship. Your brother never goes to the property. Your spouse expects to get the property if something should happen to you. The titling of the property, however, makes it clear: The brother inherits it. Titling involves not only real estate and vehicles but also bank and investment accounts.

A will only comes into play when assets don't have a title or a beneficiary. Those two things reign supreme over a will. It's not the other way around. Most people don't realize that. They think they can write something in a will to override, for example, a deed. They cannot. The will is the catch-all. You could bequeath all of your assets to your favorite pet, but if your house is titled jointly with someone, your will doesn't override that. Nor does it override the beneficiary on a life insurance policy. It is crucial to understand how assets, property, and accounts are registered, how they are titled, and what the impact would be in the event of death.

Besides serving as a catch-all, a will also can address your wishes on a wide variety of matters. Who will take care of your minor children? What will be done with your remains? The will can include trust language that talks about the distribution of property for the children, even adult children. The language can be simple or complex, depending on the nature of what you wish to accomplish.

Instead of a will, you might put what you own into a revocable living trust, which essentially will distribute it however you want. The trust also can be a means by which you hold assets. Even so, you typically have a will that refers to the trust (or vice versa).

In general, your planning process needs to include a legacy review exercise. Working with an attorney, we can map out in visual format the flow so that you understand who is in charge, who is making decisions, and where things are going.

It is not uncommon for people to be surprised to find that what is written on a document is not what they intended. Or as I explain it to clients: After ten Thanksgiving dinners, you're wondering what in the world you were thinking when you named your brother-in-law as your personal representative or as the guardian of your children. You need to intentionally plan for the care of children, disabled family members, stepchildren and adopted children, parents, and your partner or spouse.

BELOW THE GRASS PLANNING™

When we discuss legal planning for after death, we refer to it as "below-the-grass" planning. (Earlier, we discussed above-the-grass legal planning for your affairs before death.) Following is a summary of some specific elements of below-the-grass planning:

- Last Will & Testament
  - Testamentary Trusts
  - Disclaimer Trusts
  - Marital, Credit Shelter, Family and/or Bypass Trusts
  - Qualified Terminal Interest Property Trusts (QTIP)
  - Conduit Trusts
  - Tax-Sensitive Language Review
- Irrevocable Life Insurance Trusts (ILIT)
- Charitable Lead Trusts (CLAT)
- Charitable Remainder Annuity Trusts (CRAT)
- Charitable Remainder Unitrusts (CRUT)

Estate planning involves more than just arranging for the disposition of your money and other assets when you die. It should be done in tandem with above-the-grass planning. You should make advance provisions to transfer control to someone else, either temporarily or permanently, for financial, legal, and medical matters.

We live in a society that tries to protect everybody's interests. It might not always be convenient in a time of crisis, but those protections do serve a purpose. I think it's imparative to make sure you designate somebody to act on your behalf if you cannot. You need such foundational legal documents as durable powers of attorney and health-care directives. They are not expensive to set up, and they are invaluable when you need them.

THE FLOW OF YOUR LEGACY

Consider this: If your children are adults and they inherit several million dollars of assets through retirement plans, life insurance, etc., are they mature enough to handle the money on their own?

Even if your answer is yes, you may still want some control over the distribution of that money. You may wish to protect your heirs against divorcing spouses or creditors or their own spendthrift tendencies.

In developing your own documents, have thorough discussions with your estate planning attorney. The legal community tends to establish a default as to when assets should be distributed to a child, such as at age 25.

My observations have convinced me that a major inheritance can derail the path that a young person might take. He or she is being called upon for the first time to manage a large sum of money and may simply lack the ability or maturity. At any age, that can be a challenge. Statistics show it is not unusual for lottery millionaires to be broke after a year or two. Leaving a sizable sum to an heir calls for careful consideration and planning. Even if an adult child is financially responsible, circumstances in their lives at the time of inheritance could take control of all, or at least part, of what you intended as a gift. Among those circumstances are divorcing spouses, creditors, lawsuits, and bankruptcy.

Through a will, you can do a lot to direct your resources to help the causes, charities, places of worship, and people you care about. There are many ways that you can structure such giving, and it doesn't have to be complex. A professional can guide you on the best route.

We assist our clients in the coordination of such matters with an attorney, and we prepare what we call a "legacy flow" for the client and attorney to review. A legacy flow basically shows who is responsible and how, for the various elements of a client's legal plan. In effect, the review translates a long, wordy, and boring document into a visual format so that people can see what will happen in a variety of scenarios.

In the anatomy of a financial plan, each of the elements supports the others. One flows into the next. That's why it's so incredibly important to have somebody who understands this and is weaving the thread of continuity among all of the disciplines. Through diligent and comprehensive attention to your financial plan, you no longer will feel the need to keep up with the Joneses. In fact, I'm confident they will eventually be unable to keep up with you.

EPILOGUE

TO SWIM WITH MANTAS

After a kiss under the Eiffel Tower, Beth and I began to plan our wedding. We decided on an intimate, weeklong gathering of about 30 family members and close friends on the Hawaiian island of Kona. Our reception was a luau at the Hilton Waikoloa Village.

And it was on Kona that I swam with the mantas.

It was something I had long wanted to do, and my new bride arranged it for us. I had learned to dive as a cadet at the military academy. A good friend became a master diver in Guam, and we had some great outings. We often talked about swimming with the mantas in Micronesia, but I never got the chance.

Now, as these majestic gentle giants swirled above me, I felt a deep sense of accomplishment. I knew this was where I needed to be. It was a feeling of what life could be. I'd known it before, and I will know it always, through all the ebbs and flows. This was a momer of abundance. This was a moment of joy. This was a "Living my Ideal Life" moment.

In my faith, I know that God has been setting up the big plan all along. His script for my life hasn't been what I expected. It's that way for most of us. I may never understand why Theresa had to leave so early. I don't necessarily need to know. I do know that after that door closed, this one opened, wide and wonderfully.

I think, often, of those doors in my life. Of my mother's decision to keep me and raise me. Of my grandparents' and stepfather's welcoming arms. Of the wall tumbling down in Berlin as I was falling in love. And of falling in love again.

I think my life has been about determining what I really wanted and figuring out how to make it happen and living life to the fullest. I believe I have learned grace. I feel far more accepting of individuals and their choices, whether family, friends, or clients. I look for the "why" behind the "what."

None of us really knows whether we will have tomorrow. And while I believe that there is a definite need to plan for the future, you may be planning for a future that never arrives. I'm not saying we should live as if tomorrow will never come. That's foolish. But I also see the folly in living life as if tomorrow is guaranteed.

Each of us, I believe, needs to strike a balance—and you can find that balance when you understand what is truly important to you. We must be true to our values. That, in essence, is what financial planning is all about. For me, those values are faith, family, and friends. As a financial planner, I wish to practice what I preach.

CPSIA information can be obtained at www.ICGtesting.com
Printed in the USA
BVOW08s0655090615

403814BV00024B/249/P